Blissology

donlast.com

About the Author

Andy Baggott is a healer, spiritual teacher, and the author of thirteen books. He runs a busy healing practice from his home in England, lectures and teaches, and has been interviewed on television and radio. For more information, visit him online at www.andy baggott.com.

Blissology

The Art & Science of Happiness

Andy Baggott

Llewellyn Publications
Woodbury, Minnesota

First Edition
Second Printing, 2011

Cover design by Adrienne Zimiga
Cover image © Kirsty Pargeter/Alamy

Llewellyn is a registered trademark of Llewellyn Worldwide Ltd.

Library of Congress Cataloging-in-Publication Data
Baggott, Andy.
  Blissology : the art & science of happiness / Andy Baggott.—1st ed.
    p. cm.
  Includes bibliographical references (p.   ).
  ISBN 978-0-7387-2004-3
  1. Happiness—Miscellanea. 2. Success—Psychic aspects. I. Title.
  BF1999.B245 2011
  158—dc22
                                    2010038833

Llewellyn Worldwide Ltd. does not participate in, endorse, or have any authority or responsibility concerning private business transactions between our authors and the public.
    All mail addressed to the author is forwarded but the publisher cannot, unless specifically instructed by the author, give out an address or phone number.
    Any Internet references contained in this work are current at publication time, but the publisher cannot guarantee that a specific location will continue to be maintained. Please refer to the publisher's website for links to authors' websites and other sources.

Llewellyn Publications
A Division of Llewellyn Worldwide Ltd.
2143 Wooddale Drive
Woodbury, MN 55125-2989
www.llewellyn.com

Printed in the United States of America

This book is dedicated to you, the reader,
in celebration of your inner beauty and happiness.

Contents

STEP THREE

Living Happiness

Acknowledgements

Thanks to my agent, Susan Mears, and to all the lovely people at Llewellyn for sharing in my vision and bringing it to fruition. Great appreciation goes to all the wise men and women whose inspiring words are quoted throughout this book. Thanks also to Eli, Snorkey, Larraine, Jess, and Tilly for their continual support and friendship, especially during the writing of this book. Thanks also to all the wonderful people I have met over the many years I have been treading this amazing path of happiness. You have all deepened my joy. I must also acknowledge the many teachers I have both met and read, especially Esther and Jerry Hicks whose wonderful work with Abraham continues to inspire me. Thanks especially to them for the "wouldn't it be nice" game—it changed my life. I would like to express my deep thanks and appreciation for the tireless support, endless encouragement, and creative input from my wife,

Debbie. Her sense of fun and play kept me on track, and so often showed me a more beautiful way of expressing my ideas. Without her, this book would not have been written.

Introduction

Wouldn't it be nice if, from this moment on, your life consistently improved in ways beyond your wildest dreams? *Blissology* is all about making that happen right here and now. I combine cutting-edge science with the accumulated wisdom of some of the world's deepest and oldest spiritual traditions to present you with compelling evidence that you can become the master of your own life and destiny.

We each have more control over our lives and how we feel than most of us realize. Blissology shows you how to claim this control for yourself, and in doing so, release your latent potential to create the life of your dreams. You can have the life you want—and you can have it now. The key lies in taking full responsibility. By doing so, you begin to understand that the power to change your life lies solely within your hands.

This book is divided into four sections, each section representing a steppingstone toward the life of your dreams. The first section is about understanding the true nature of happiness and how you can achieve it in your life. You will learn about some of the latest scientific discoveries regarding happiness and about the simple philosophy behind achieving your goals. In the second section, I provide simple yet powerful tools to immediately bring more happiness into your life. In the third section, I share my ideas for becoming the master creator of your own reality and bringing about the real changes you desire. The final section is about sharing your newfound deeper happiness with those around you in order to make the world a better place. I'll show you how to keep hold of your inner calm regardless of what is happening around you, and how to teach others, through your shining example, to achieve the same thing for themselves.

This is a real, hands-on approach, so you don't need to take great leaps of faith or radically change your beliefs in order to achieve a better life. You simply have to pick up the tools and try them for yourself. Once you see how accessible this wisdom is, your faith, your belief in yourself, and your ability to manifest positive change will deepen. Very soon you'll be wondering if there's a limit to how fulfilling your life can become.

Your most powerful ally on your journey to happiness is your own mind. When you harness the mind to seek out happiness, you not only improve your emotional health, you'll also bolster your physical health. Throughout this book, we'll explore many different ways to unlock the power of your own subconscious to manifest change and activate self-healing and empowerment. You will learn how to achieve inner calm quickly and efficiently, and even how to reduce physical pain. But most importantly, you will learn how to be in charge of your own life and future.

———

I am no stranger to the challenges of life. In my early twenties, I was married, father of a beautiful young daughter, and working as a manager in the leisure industry. I lived in a company house, drove a company car, and was paid a good salary. I attended some of the best social events, from horse racing at Royal Ascot to soccer's World Cup. You might think that I had a great life, but I was in fact desperately unhappy and dissatisfied. I never seemed to have enough time for enjoyment, as I was so stressed that I had long forgotten what feeling happy and relaxed was like.

Suddenly, my life began to spiral further out of control. My daughter Lara, at the age of three months, had a reaction to a vaccination, developed epilepsy, and continued to have adverse reactions to the anticonvulsant drugs the doctors gave her. This resulted in more and more frequent fits that were so long they invariably required hospitalization.

At first, I was so busy adjusting to this change that I didn't question what was happening. I assumed this was a temporary crisis and that Lara would soon get better. But she didn't. She went from one medical crisis to another. I seemed to be on a perpetual emotional roller coaster that I was powerless to stop. Every time Lara came out of hospital, I hoped it would be the last time, that she would get better and that life could return to normal, but it never did. Within a few weeks, she would always fall ill again. I found myself filled with despair.

I wondered what I did to deserve such a fate—and I began to question everything in my life. I realized the money, success, and material objects I thought would make me happy were powerless to bring any lasting quality to my life. "What is it that I am missing?" I asked myself again and again. During this time of great confusion, there was only one thing I knew was real, my love for Lara. At the age of eighteen months, she had a four-and-a-half hour seizure that resulted in brain damage and a severe learning disability. She lost her ability to speak and had to relearn how to sit up, crawl, and walk. I felt utterly and terribly defeated.

At one of my lowest points, I sat by her hospital bed and wondered if it had been better if she had died. Thinking in such stark terms suddenly brought my mind into focus. It changed how I felt about everything. In that moment, nothing seemed important except loving my daughter. That was the only thing I could do to help her. I resolved that if Lara was going to die, I would make the best of my time with her—and that nothing else really mattered.

At this terrible time, my love for Lara carried me through. I discovered, to my surprise, I could actually take a lot more than I thought I could. Over the next eighteen months, her illnesses became more frequent, resulting in many sleepless nights. I became chronically sleep deprived, but my determination to be there kept me going.

I began looking for better ways of coping with life. I took up tai chi and learned how to meditate, both of which had a profound effect on me. I learned to find stillness within the storm of my life—and it felt good. I practiced tai chi every day, and the more I practiced, the better I felt. But then something else happened. In the space of three months, almost everything that I had valued in my life disappeared. I lost my job, my car, and salary; my marriage broke down; and I was evicted from my house. I suddenly found myself a penniless, homeless, single parent with a very sick child, living on state benefits in a government-sponsored shelter. I hit rock bottom.

You might think that this chain of events would have sent me spiraling into depression, but I actually felt a tremendous feeling of relief. All I really had to worry about now was me and my daughter. All my other responsibilities and commitments were gone. For the first time in years, I felt free.

This new sense of freedom brought with it new feelings of hope. Perhaps this had all happened to me for a reason. Maybe I was meant to find out how to help Lara be well. I resolved that if the doctors couldn't heal her, I would make it my mission to discover how to heal her myself.

It was obvious to me that Western medicine was making Lara worse, not better. I began my search by studying Eastern approaches to healing. I enrolled in college courses to learn acupuncture and complementary medicine and discovered a different perspective to health and healing—one that revolved around personal responsibility. Filled with a newfound enthusiasm, I changed my diet, my lifestyle, and my destructive ways of thinking. As I made these changes, I found that my quality of life improved dramatically. My thirst for knowledge became insatiable. I read book after book about healing, alternative medicine, and Eastern spiritual practices. The learning came easily. In the space of a few months, my life changed beyond recognition, as if I had suddenly woken from a bad dream. I felt a new passion for living and a deep sense that my destiny was in my own hands. Every spare minute I was not caring for Lara, I would study and practice new healing techniques.

Lara's life changed too. I weaned her off her drugs and began treating her with natural medicines and whole foods. The change in her was remarkable. Her convulsive fits reduced dramatically in both frequency and length, and she stopped getting infections. What was even more thrilling was that she began to laugh and play like a normal child. It was as if she, too, was waking up to a new life.

After three years of study, I began my clinical practice in acupuncture and developed a busy practice. At the same time, I met my current wife and together we embarked on a journey to discover deeper levels of happiness. My life had turned around and I started to wonder just how far I could take it.

Over the next few years, as I continued my search, I met some truly remarkable people. I studied with masters from many different spiritual traditions, including Native American, Celtic, South American, Taoist, and Buddhist. Each encounter took me deeper into my understanding of myself and my place within this amazing universe. I also studied with a variety of healers and learned about traditional herbalism, naturopathy, and natural nutrition. As my knowledge grew, I applied it to myself and then to Lara. By the time she was eight years old, she was free of all medication and also of serious illness. In fact, she enjoys exceptional health and has not had any kind of serious infection in the past fourteen years.

I continued to see clients, finding that they increasingly came to me wanting more than just improved health—they wanted a better quality of life. I began sharing my own understanding of how to achieve that. I showed them how to take personal responsibility and empower themselves with simple tools to focus their attention on happiness and healing. I saw people change their lives and connect with lasting happiness, and this in turn expanded my own sense of well-being.

In recent years, my research and has taken me into the world of quantum physics and cellular biochemistry. Surprisingly, I found that this new knowledge fit perfectly with so much of what I had learned on my spiritual journey. I also became interested in the work of Esther and Jerry Hicks, which expanded my horizons, gave me wonderful new tools to play with, and deepened my sense of inner well-being beyond what I thought was possible. Today, my life is full, rich, and abundant. I feel truly blessed to have experienced all that I have. Both good and bad, it has led me to achieve an ever-deepening sense of happiness and joy.

———

In this book I share much of what I have discovered on my path through life. Over the many years I have been working with this wisdom, it has consistently improved and expanded my own quality of life and the lives of the many people I have shared it with so far. I make some big claims about the nature of the universe and your place within it that you might find hard to accept. I suggest you don't just take what I say on faith, but put it to the test. Try the techniques and see for yourself their power to bring about positive change in your own life. Throughout this book, I share stories from my work with clients. Although I have changed the names and certain details to protect anonymity, the essence of every story is true.

Achieving true happiness takes both understanding and skill, but there is nothing complex about the process. In my experience, the only thing that prevents people from finding it for themselves is its simplicity; so perhaps your greatest work will come in letting go of past beliefs and complex thinking.

Blissology is about improving the quality of your life on every level. Both a science and an art, our journey will allow us to explore the many aspects of who we are and who we can become. We will draw inspiration from the latest scientific discoveries as well as ancient wisdom—and, in doing so, broaden our understanding and expand our creativity. We will tell a new story of who we are and where we are going. We will explore the physical, the metaphysical, our divinity, and what this means for us living in this current space-time reality we call "the present." Long before you reach the end of this book, you will come to the undeniable conclusion that, when we reconnect with who we really are, happiness becomes as normal as breathing.

Step One

Understanding Happiness

The journey begins

The journey of a thousand miles begins with one step.

LAO TSU

Everybody wants to be happy, but few people understand how to achieve this consistently. It is easy to be happy when things are going well, but when we face challenging times, most people slip from happiness into stress. Blissology teaches a different approach to life—one that allows you to find happiness and keep hold of it in any situation.

What makes Blissology different is that it is a fusion of both art *and* science. In the West, art and science are often regarded as polar opposites because they employ two different ways of thinking. Science uses logic and deduction to arrive at a conclusion, whereas art requires imagination. In terms of problem solving, the scientist starts with the problem and works out the steps required to solve it. The artist, on the other hand, starts by imagining the solution and then seeks out resources to match that solution.

Ancient wisdom teaches that science and art are two sides of the same coin, and that a happy, healthy, and fulfilling life is achieved through a combination of both. In order to achieve anything, we need to clearly see our goal while also understanding the steps required to realize it. Focus solely on your goal and you are in danger of getting lost in fanciful pipe dreams; focus solely on the steps you need to take and you may lose sight of your goal. Only when you have a vision and are able to consistently walk toward it, will that vision be realized.

Happiness is the birthright of every human being on this planet. It is a state of being in which we are in touch with our true inner nature and fully connected to our inner wisdom. This wisdom is held in every cell of your body within your DNA. Most people have heard of the double helix of DNA that holds our genetic information, but this accounts for only 10 percent of our total DNA. Scientists originally believed that the double helix was the only active part of our genetic code and subsequently labeled the rest as "junk." However, in more recent years some startling discoveries have been made about this other 90 percent. The most notable is the work by Russian biophysicist and molecular biologist Pjotr Garjajev and his colleagues (www .rexresearch.com/gajarev/gajarev.htm). They explored the vibrational behavior of DNA and found that living chromosomes function just like a holographic computer.

Stored within this highly sophisticated DNA biocomputer is all the accumulated wisdom of our ancestors. Each of us holds ancient memories—memories that science is just beginning to uncover. Although still in its infancy, scientists studying genetics can already map your ancestry back to between ten thousand and forty-five thousand years ago. Bryan Sykes, an Oxford-based genetic researcher, has traced European female genetic lines back to just seven common, post-ice age ancestresses. His best-selling book, *The Seven Daughters of Eve*, explains how each of us can trace our genetic ancestors back thousands of years.

Every cell of your body contains your DNA and is a storehouse of deep and profound ancestral wisdom. Imagine having access to the life experiences of thousands of different people who have all led varied lives. That would give you an awareness of how to navigate through life in a manner that, to others, might appear almost divine. Every human being can access this wisdom if they know how.

You hold within your consciousness the memory of the many, many journeys you have yourself lived on your path from the past to the present. This path began long before you were born—even before the dawn of time. Scientists tell us that all the energy within our universe is eternal. If energy is eternal and your consciousness is part of that energy, then doesn't that also make you an eternal being? The energy that is now a part of you existed even before the Big Bang!

Virtually all religions teach that when we die, our consciousness returns to its source. So what is this source? In her book *The Field*, Lynne McTaggart describes something called the "Zero Point Field." Over the past one hundred or so years, scientists have been accumulating evidence for the existence of an energy field that connects everything in our universe. It is a dynamic interconnected web of energy and is the source of all that exists in our physical world. Ancient people have been describing this field and the energy that flows from it for thousands of years. God, the Great Spirit, chi, prana, and the Web of Life are just some of the many terms that have been used to describe this source of all life. We shall simply call it *Source Energy*.

Source Energy is like a swirling soup of infinite possibilities. If we can tap into it, we can begin to choose which possibilities we want to manifest into our lives. Your parents created your physical shell, but you are so much more than that. You are, in fact, your own creator and also the creator of your unfolding reality. You have the ability to be the master of your own destiny and choose exactly what kinds of experiences you want—the life you want to live and the kind of people you want to share that life with. What's more, happiness is the key that unlocks this ability.

This might sound like the stuff of fairy tales, but it is not. By applying the simple tools and exercises shared within this book, you can become the master creator of your own reality. How would you really like your life to be? Wouldn't you like your life to be a great adventure with each experience taking you to new levels of understanding, deeper levels of bliss, and a forever-expanding sense of appreciation? It is your destiny to experience life this way, should you so choose.

Your destiny is not some preordained path filled with challenges that you must overcome in order to earn the right to be happy. It is the path that you take as you stand on the leading edge of the universe and create the reality for yourself that you find most pleasing. By doing so, you become a fully conscious participant in your life and in the very expansion of the universe.

We are not just living in our universe—we are an active part of it. Our thoughts and feelings mold our reality. Only by focusing within and changing our patterns of thought and behavior can we have any real influence on our lives. Change yourself and you change your reality. Feel better within yourself and it will be reflected back to you a thousand times in your unfolding life. So let's step forward into a new way of being.

Who's in charge of how you feel?

I say, follow your bliss and don't be afraid, and doors will open where you didn't know they were going to be.

JOSEPH CAMPBELL

As an acupuncturist and healer, I help people rediscover their health, and one of the most important prerequisites for health is happiness. Seeing a client find the self-trust and empowerment to seek their own health and happiness is always a bliss-filled experience for both of us. A fundamental step on the journey to bliss is the realization that we—and we alone—are in charge of how we think and feel. Although this self-determination lies at the core of understanding happiness, very often it takes a surprising and unexpected turn of events for people to discover this truth.

The first time I met Helen, she arrived at my clinic looking far from healthy and happy. She hobbled along with the help of two walking sticks and looked very tired and miserable. She struggled to get up the step at my front door, despite it being only a couple of inches high. I helped her into my treatment room and onto a chair. She sat down with a big sigh and promptly burst into tears.

As we spoke it became obvious to me that she was very depressed. She was only in her late fifties but, six years previously, she had been diagnosed with multiple sclerosis, which had a devastating effect on her life. Her mobility and balance were very poor, she was in constant pain despite the best efforts of her doctors to find drugs that did not give her terrible side effects, and, as she explained, she was tired of living. Over the course of two hours, she told me her story and I shared with her a vision of the possibility of becoming well again. No one had ever suggested to her that she could get better.

We began working together, empowering her to reclaim her health. We made some significant changes to her diet, I gave her regular acupuncture to help with her pain, and, most importantly, I began showing her some simple tools and exercises that she could use to focus on feeling better. Over the next few months she began to turn her life around. She discovered that the more she focused on things that made her feel good, the more her symptoms subsided. Her balance improved, her pain decreased dramatically, and she soon was able to walk without the aid of her sticks. For the first time in six years she found hope and began to dream of a brighter future. I saw her every week and, little by little, she got better and better.

Then one day she arrived at my door with a walking stick in each hand again. She told me that her "relapse" had happened the day before and that she could see no reason for it.

"It's a complete mystery," she told me.

"What did you do the previous evening?" I asked her.

"Oh, nothing out of the ordinary," she replied. "I just sat with my husband and watched TV for a couple of hours and then went to bed."

It did indeed appear to be a mystery until I asked her what she had watched. Suddenly her whole demeanor changed. She screwed up her face and growled, "My husband insisted on watching the football. I *hate* football."

For two hours she had sat with her husband feeling nothing but hatred. It had not occurred to her that she could do anything else. I told her that I felt the stress of sitting for two hours feeling hatred was the cause of her relapse. Once she realized that her husband did not care if she sat with him through the football game, and that she could go and do something that felt much better to her, she never had such a relapse again.

It is not what we experience in life that dictates our happiness, but how we respond to these experiences. Some people think that circumstances or the words of others have the power to make us happy or sad, but this is not true. Situations can make us feel unhappy but only if we allow them to do so. You and you alone are in charge of how you feel, and you always have the choice to change how you feel. You can do this either by changing how you think or by choosing to do something different that feels better.

To be upset is a choice that we alone make, either consciously or subconsciously. If we understand that we are each in charge of our own feelings, then we will also realize that only we hold the power to change those feelings. Every human being holds within them this power to change sadness into joy, fear into trust, and anxiety into hope. Choose to feel better. When you choose a better feeling, your body will respond.

Three relaxing breaths

*Sometimes the most important thing in a whole day
is the rest we take between two deep breaths.*

ETTY HILLESUM

Here is a simple Taoist meditation technique that, with practice, will enable you to find balance and the power to deal with any kind of situation. It only takes about thirty seconds to do and you can apply it anytime, anywhere— even while driving. Nothing feels better than when you are *in the zone*. You feel calm and in control, alert, and ready to deal with any situation. In Taoist meditation, the two primary guidelines are *jing* (quiet, stillness, calm) and *ding* (concentration, focus). These are the same two characteristics required for being in the zone.

There are two versions of this exercise: the first for normal situations and the second for exceptional situations.

Three relaxing breaths—version one

You can use this technique to help you through any kind of change in your life. It is especially useful just before a required change of mood, such as prior to public speaking or before mediation.

1. Sit or stand with your mouth closed and your tongue gently resting on your upper palate.

2. Take a slow, deep breath in through your nose. Breathe right down into your abdomen, feeling it expand so that your lungs fill completely. As you breathe in, imagine your mind becoming alert and clear.

3. Hold the breath for a moment.

4. Exhale slowly through your nose. As you exhale, imagine any stress flowing easily out of your body.

5. Hold your lungs empty for a moment.

6. Repeat steps 2 through 5 twice.

7. Say to yourself, "I am calm and alert."

Three relaxing breaths—version two

Use this technique whenever you experience any kind of shock or emotional upset.

1. Sit or stand with your mouth closed and your tongue gently resting on your upper palate.

2. Take a slow, deep breath in through your nose.

3. Hold the breath for a moment.

4. Blow out slowly through your mouth. As you exhale, imagine all feelings of unease flowing easily out of your body.

5. Hold your lungs empty for a moment.

6. Repeat steps 2 through 5 twice.

7. Say to yourself, "I am calm and alert."

These techniques are effective because when people become stressed, they tend to restrict their breathing. This starves the brain of vital oxygen, which in turn, clouds their thinking. Just three relaxing breaths will clear your mind, help you access your inner wisdom and show you the best path to take.

The root of unhappiness

The greatest happiness is to know the source of unhappiness.
FYODOR DOSTOEVSKY

Sir Isaac Newton was one of the founding fathers of classical physics. His theories are still used to explain much of what unfolds in our physical universe. The movement of planets around stars and the manner in which all physical matter interacts can be neatly explained with a variety of mathematical equations. These equations so accurately predict how physical matter interacts that they are today called the Laws of Physics. However, when quantum physicists began to study the subatomic world, they found that these laws no longer applied. A planet remains in a relatively stable orbit around a star because of gravity; however, at the subatomic level, scientists were not dealing with physical objects but little pockets of positive and negative charge on which gravity has no influence. Without gravity, the Laws of Physics are redundant.

The most fundamental atom in our universe is the hydrogen atom, which is made up of a nucleus consisting of a single proton holding a positive charge that is orbited by a single electron holding a negative charge. For many years, quantum physicists pondered the question of what force keeps the electron in a stable orbit around the proton. Newtonian physics predicted that sooner or later the electron would run out of energy and be drawn into the nucleus, causing the atom to collapse. The only explanation that fit was that the electron "borrows" energy from a source outside of the physical universe. This source is now called the Zero Point Field. Quantum equations mathematically show that electrons participate in a constant energy exchange with this field to maintain a state of dynamic equilibrium that keeps them in a stable orbit.

As quantum physicists delved deeper into the world of the very small, they made an even more remarkable discovery. They found that subatomic particles are forever popping in and out of existence. One of the most famous claims of quantum physics is that subatomic particles most often exist most as waves of possibility rather than as distinct objects, and that only when you try to observe and measure a particle does this wave of possibility collapse into a single particle. But if these particles do pop in and out of existence, where do they go when they are not here? The answer once again is the Zero Point Field. This field is quite literally the source of all matter, and it is the location of the nonphysical reality that we call Source Energy.

Before anything comes into physical existence, it "lives" in the nonphysical reality of Source Energy. The greatest part of all of creation exists in the nonphysical, including you and me. The concept of energy, like the concept of God, is that it is eternal. Energy has always existed and will always exist. You are I are a part of that energy, so we too must be eternal. Esther and Jerry Hicks write about this in their book *Ask and It Is Given*. They imply that our physical lives are finite, but our consciousness is infinite and spends a majority of its time in Source Energy. The Hicks say that even now the greatest part of who you really are is in Source Energy. Just as subatomic particles pop in and out of existence, so do we. We "pop" into existence for a lifetime, return to Source Energy when we die, only to "pop" back into physical reality again for another lifetime. If this is true, it means that there is no death, only life in the physical, followed by life in the nonphysical, followed by life in the physical, and so on.

Our universe is without fault. It is always perfectly balanced in a state of dynamic equilibrium. Likewise, there is actually nothing wrong with you. Your life is just a mirror of how you currently choose to play with the energies and situations you attract toward you. An endless stream of well-being flows throughout our universe, and if we want a better life, all we have to do is tap into it. Source Energy is that stream.

Unhappiness has no source except within ourselves and is nothing more or less than a disconnection from happiness—a disconnection from the flow of positivity eternally emanating from Source Energy. We are eternal beings of pure positive energy, and the only reason we don't feel that way is because we have become disconnected. We have turned off our own light. Blissology offers each of us the tools to reconnect with who we really are and reconnect with happiness, which is our most natural state of being.

The anatomy and physiology
of happiness

Happiness cannot come from without.
It must come from within.

HELEN KELLER

Neuroscience, the study of the nervous system, was still in its infancy when a naïve but ambitious young woman named Candace Pert enrolled in the Johns Hopkins Medical School's pharmacology department. At twenty-four-years old and married with a young son, she was filled with the enthusiasm of youth and a burning desire to make a difference. Her professor, Sol Snyder, was even more ambitious, with a reputation for being the rebel of pharmacology. He viewed science as a game to be won and fellow scientists in his field of expertise as competitors to be beaten. He took Pert under his wing and taught her both his scientific methodologies and his wisdom.

"Always trust your hunches," he told her.

Her research involved the study of receptors, the sense organs of the cell. The outer membrane of every cell in the body has these receptors—and up to seventy different types. They keep the cell in touch with what is happening in the body as a whole. For instance, if the body is dehydrated, this is felt at a cellular level via these receptors. A single cell can have tens, or even hundreds, of thousands of these receptors. They lie dormant until a small molecule, called a *ligand*, binds to that receptor and makes it active.

In her groundbreaking book, *The Molecules of Emotion: The Science Behind Mind-Body Medicine*, Pert describes her favorite category of ligand, *peptides*, as follows: "If the cell is the engine that drives all life, then the receptors are the buttons on the control panel of that engine and the specific peptide (or other ligand) is the finger that pushes the button and gets things started." Each specific peptide has a unique effect on how we feel at a cellular level.

Early on, she worked on trying to isolate the opiate receptor using morphine, but after several failed trials Sol Snyder ordered her to stop looking and focus on other work. Following a hunch, she disobeyed him, went behind his back, and, using his laboratory's funds, ordered a fresh batch of a different opiate to continue her work. Fortunately, Pert was successful, and when she shared her discovery with Snyder, rather than being annoyed, he assigned a technician to help her. Within weeks, she published her findings in the prestigious *Science* journal. Her innovative work opened up the possibility for the discovery of many other key receptors and a deeper understanding of how cells and the brain communicate with one another. This in turn radically changed our understanding of how our feelings and biochemistry are intrinsically linked.

The feeling of happiness is created in the body by a part of the brain called the hypothalamus, a small region of the brain about the size of a cherry that lies just above the pituitary gland. The hypothalamus has many different functions, one of its most vital is the control of the sympathetic nervous system. Through this system, it has nerve connections to most other regions of the nervous system. In response to stressful situations, the hypothalamus initiates sympathetic nervous system activity such as increasing heart rate, widening the pupils (to be able to take in more visual information), increasing breathing rate, and directing extra blood flow to the muscles. These processes are collectively known as the "fight or flight" response.

Other groups of nerve cells in the hypothalamus are concerned with the regulation of brain temperature, and hence, the regulation of overall body temperature. When blood flow to the brain is hotter or cooler than is normal, the hypothalamus responds by directing the body to release or create heat through sweating or shivering. Another role of this remarkable part of the brain is in the coordination between the nervous and endocrine (hormonal) systems. The hypothalamus converts nerve signals into hormonal signals that are sent to the pituitary gland, which in turn directs the appropriate responses in the rest of the endocrine system (e.g., to the pancreas to regulate blood sugar and to the adrenals and thyroid to regulate body metabolism).

In relation to our emotions, the hypothalamus manufactures peptides (protein fragments of small-chain amino acid sequences using two or more different amino acids) to match the emotion we currently feel. There are peptides for happiness, anger, guilt, envy, sadness, and every other feeling on the emotional scale. Think about this for a moment—there is a chemical messenger that matches our every emotional state. The moment we feel an emotion, the hypothalamus assembles peptides that are released through the pituitary into the bloodstream and from there they travel to different centers of the body.

Every single cell within your amazing biostructure has receptors on its surface for these peptides. Different cells in different regions of the body have varying distributions of these receptors. Some have only a few, and others have literally thousands. When peptides are released into the bloodstream (and they are released in millions), each one is like a key trying to find a lock to fit into. The specific receptors that match these peptides remain inactive on the outer cell membrane until the appropriate peptide comes along and fits the lock. When this happens, a pathway into the cell is opened, initiating a cascade of biochemical responses that acts like a wave of shifting consciousness rippling from each cell throughout the body.

Every moment of every day you are changing at a cellular level. Often the changes are subtle, so that we do not notice them, but if, for instance, we are sexually aroused or witness something shocking, the response can be huge and cause a dramatic change in how we are feeling and reacting. We are emotional beings and, whether or not we realize it, we respond emotionally to every situation that manifests into our lives. The problem many people have is that they habitually access negative emotions. The hypothalamus responds to how we feel, so if we feel depressed every day when we wake up, our hypothalamus will produce peptides to match those feelings and these messengers will spread throughout the body, thus reinforcing how we feel. This in turn puts us in an emotional and physiological state that is totally conducive to feeling more of the same emotion. We get locked into a cycle of negative feelings that seems impossible to break out of, and our very physical body reinforces it.

The only way to break this cycle is to begin to feel happier. Once you begin to feel happier, you produce *bliss peptides*, which create a greater overall feeling of well-being. This, of course, leads to more feelings of happiness, which means producing even more peptides and so on until you are overflowing with joy. It is really very simple—if you can learn to feel happy habitually, it will become your day-to-day reality. Then you will seek out experiences that reinforce those feelings and life will become the adventure of the forever-expanding experience that we all desire. Not only that, you will be so much better equipped to deal with life's challenges in a positive way.

Practicing feeling happier moment by moment is the key to understanding happiness and living in bliss. No matter how you are currently feeling, no matter what your state of health, finances, or relationships with others, you have to decide to start feeling good about life right here and now. So many people say "I will be happy when..." or "I would be happy if..." but to say this keeps happiness locked into the future—always far away from the now, and never a reality. If you want to be happy, sooner or later *you* have to decide to start feeling happy *now*, no matter what your life is like. If you can start to feel better about life, life will get better. If you remain addicted to your negative emotions, your physical body reinforces that ,and you live life as a pawn of fate rather than the creator of your own reality.

The hypothalamus responds to how you feel and brings the body into alignment with that feeling. Change your feelings and you change everything within every cell of your body, including pH, temperature, hydration, cell membrane potential, and the magnetic vibration you emit. This literally changes your whole reality and opens up new possibilities for change that once only existed as distant potentialities within Source Energy. Change your feelings and Source Energy responds to bring new possibilities into your reality. Understand happiness and your whole life can change.

The Law of Attraction

The most beautiful thing we can experience is the mysterious.
It is the source of all true art and all science.

ALBERT EINSTEIN

The universe is governed by an unfailing principle called the *Law of Attraction*. It is what forms galaxies, planets, and even you and me. It ensures that everything in our universe remains in order. Consider this: Carbon is the basic building block of life. It is the most dominant part of all living matter. The pages of this book were once part of a living tree and are still predominantly composed of carbon. What stops the carbon atoms of this page from becoming mixed up with the carbon atoms that make up your body? The answer is the Law of Attraction.

Esther and Jerry Hicks, in their best-selling book *Ask and It Is Given,* describe the Law of Attraction as follows: "That which is like unto itself is drawn." What this means is that any vibration will attract to itself similar vibrations. Quantum physics tells us that the universe is composed of vibrating pockets of energy and the Law of Attraction explains how these pockets of energy join together to form matter. Your atoms all have a similar vibration, like a distinct signature. The pages of this book also have their own signature. By the Law of Attraction, only vibrations with similar signatures will be attracted to one another. What does this mean when applied to happiness? It means that how we think and feel will attract situations and events that match those thoughts and feelings. Quite literally like a magnet, what you give your attention to dictates what you will attract into your life.

So many people are unaware of what they are actually giving their attention to and, more importantly, how that is making them feel. Only when we become self-aware can we hope to bring about real change in our lives. If you are feeling emotional pain, the situations you attract into your life will keep bringing that pain to the surface until you heal it. If you want to change your life, you have to change your feelings. In doing so, you will find healing and balance.

There is a whole range of feelings we experience in our lives. Think about any subject and it will evoke a feeling. How does work make you feel? Some people love their jobs and find deep fulfillment in their work, whereas others feel the exact opposite. Do you have fun in your spare time or just sit in front of the television feeling bored or frustrated? If you want to bring improvement to any area of your life, the key is to first identify how you feel about it and then seek out better feelings. The Law of Attraction will bring change to you in the form of new experiences that match your improved state of mind.

Source Energy is a field of limitless possibilities, and our thoughts and feelings are constantly calling to us the possibilities that most closely match them. The moment you say to yourself, "I want something different," you open up new possibilities that before were not available to you. The moment you consider creating the life of your dreams, it instantly becomes possible for you.

To manifest great things in your life, you have to do two things: first, ask, and second, consistently bring yourself into alignment with the stream of well-being that flows from Source Energy. Whenever you ask for anything, the universe always answers. It moves its energies to bring about what you have asked for in the most efficient manner possible. Hold that thought, and after some time it will become real. It works every time in every situation. Harness the tools to utilize this law and you become the master of your life.

The power of visualization

Imagination disposes of everything; it creates beauty, justice, and happiness, which are everything in this world.

BLAISE PASCAL

Many of the exercises in this book require the use of your imagination. Visualization is your most potent tool for changing how you feel. Some people find it easier to do than others, but with practice, anyone can become an expert in visualizing. Here are four simple exercises of increasing difficulty that you can practice in order to hone your visualization skills. Begin each exercise by closing your eyes and taking three relaxing breaths.

1. **Something familiar**. Start by imagining a room that is very familiar to you, such as your bedroom or office. Recall how the furniture is arranged, the color of the walls, the view from the window, and so on. Fill in as many different details as you can.

2. **Objects**. Imagine an object. Start with something simple like a box. What size and color is it? What is it made from? It there anything inside it? Once you can clearly see the object in your mind's eye, move on to a more complex object, such as a house. It can be any house, real or imaginary. Take a virtual walk

around and inside it, noting everything you see. Try to focus the images clearly in your mind.

3. **People**. Imagine your closest friend. Visualize him or her performing an everyday task, such as cooking or talking on the telephone. Fill in as much detail as possible about your friend's clothes, the time of day, the location, etc. Once you can imagine your best friend clearly, move on to less familiar people, such as the sales assistant in your local store.

4. **Yourself**. Start by imagining yourself standing in front of a mirror. Look at your features, expression, clothes, and surroundings. If you find this difficult, actually stand and look at yourself in a mirror before trying this exercise again. Once you can visualize yourself clearly, imagine doing something familiar, such as walking down your street or driving a car. Finally, imagine yourself doing something extraordinary, such a parachuting out of a plane. Take note of not only what you are imagining, but of how you feel.

With practice you will find that you can visualize about anything, anywhere, and anytime, even with your eyes open. You will be able to visualize while waiting for a bus, driving a car, or cooking a meal. You can imagine feelings, as well as people and events. You will also discover that you can instantly change any detail of your visualization with a simple thought. The clearer you can imagine, the faster you will see results when you use the other exercises in this book.

Practicing Happiness

Leaving the past for a brighter future

The happiness that is genuinely satisfying is accompanied by the fullest exercise of our faculties and the fullest realization of the world in which we live.

BERTRAND RUSSELL

Everyone has their own story, one that is filled with a rich variety of experiences. When we make a new acquaintance, we often exchange tales from our lives—something humans have been doing since the development of language. These exchanges are potentially very valuable because they expand our knowledge and enable us to draw on the experience of others. However, they can also be potentially detrimental, especially if the story exchanged is one that evokes negative emotions.

Of course, because the story you relay can spark the same positive or negative feelings, the path to happiness begins with telling a new story about who you are and where you are going. The past is history and even the present is just a moment in time; the future is where all the fun is. However, you cannot move toward a brighter future until you make peace with all that has been. If there are events in your past that still cause you pain, each negative feeling forms a powerful magnet of attraction and is likely to show up again and again in your life. This becomes especially true if you talk about the past in a way that doesn't actually feel good. For instance, if you say "Every spring I suffer from hay fever," you are telling a story of unending and repeated suffering. Saying it reinforces that belief. If you make statements about yourself that evoke feelings of powerlessness, pain, or suffering, they will invariably be true not only about your past, but also about your future.

Evaluating and re-evaluating yourself

This exercise will help you to take a step back and look at how you define your life. Make a list of those "absolutes" you tell yourself and carry around that defines who you are. Start with "I am ..." and then list all the words you use to describe yourself. Do you have a tendency to think of yourself in a positive way (I am optimistic, I am kind, I am hard-working, etc.) or a negative way (I am always tired, I am bored, I am stressed, etc.)?

Underline all the positive aspects about yourself. Now look at any negative aspects and change them into solutions you desire; so "I am always tired" could change to "I have boundless energy," "I am bored" to "My life is always interesting," and "I am stressed" to "I am always at ease."

Consider the information you give to others about how your life is and where you are heading. Do you have a tendency to share your hopes and dreams or your worries and fears? Write a new story based only on your positive aspects and aspirations. For instance, you might write, "I am optimistic, kind, and hard-working, and I dream of having boundless energy, new and interesting experiences, and inner peace." Only include things in your story that fill you with hope, joy, and excitement.

Many people are unaware of how they paint themselves with the story they tell. Why not try telling an inspiring story about yourself? You might be surprised at how it changes your whole perspective on life. When you tell a story that evokes positive feelings within you, you will naturally attract situations and people into your life to further expand your sense of well-being.

You can change your life right here and now because you always have the ability to *change your mind*. No matter how your life has been up until now, it can, from this moment, consistently improve. What's more, there is no limit to how good you can feel—no limit to the amount of bliss you can accumulate once you put your mind to it. Always remember that you are the most amazing and resourceful of beings; you are a natural survivor. The very fact that you are reading this book means that whatever life has thrown at you, you have come through it. You may have faced challenges, but you have always come out the other side because that *is* your natural ability.

However, if you want to ensure that history doesn't repeat itself in your life, there is a simple tool we all possess to ensure we attract new and inspiring situations into our lives. That tool is imagination, and when we apply it, we have the power to bring about real and lasting change.

Rewriting your story

This exercise shows you how to change the past so that it does not repeat itself in your future. It can be applied to any situation from your past that you found difficult, unpleasant, or challenging.

- Think back to a time in your life when you were filled with joy. Perhaps it was when you achieved something new or a time of celebration, such as a party, wedding, or the birth of a child. Remember just how good that time felt. Close your eyes, and with the power of your imagination, relive those wonderful moments. Embody those feelings.

- Now think of a time in your life that felt unpleasant and briefly recall what happened. Don't dwell on it too long, just long enough to remember how it felt.

- Use your imagination to rewrite that story in a way that feels much better. Imagine things turning out in the *best* possible way. For instance, if the event was the loss of a job, imagine getting a big promotion and becoming the star of the company. If it was an argument, imagine being loved and understood. No matter what the situation, change it into something that feels really good when you think about it. Smile to yourself as you replay the events in this new way. Embody those feelings.

- As you hold these thoughts in your mind, say to yourself, "I rewrite the past so that my future is brighter."

Congratulations! You have recalibrated your emotional magnet and this will change your reality. When you improve how you feel, you open up new possibilities for feeling even better. The more positive feelings and thoughts you hold, the more Source Energy will bring to you things that match those feelings.

———

When I was a teenager, I enjoyed cross-country running. One year I entered a race that began with a very steep and long hill. We all lined up at the start and when the gun went off, we tried to sprint to the front. After a few yards, the hill climbed steeply and most of us were reduced to walking. Puffing and panting, I looked up to see some competitors still trying to run, and all but one of them was reduced to walking. Eventually, I got to the top, and thankfully, the rest of the race was downhill. I soon got into my stride and began passing other runners. By the finish, I came in twelfth out of sixty competitors.

That evening as I lay in bed, I replayed the race in my mind. I recalled the start and all my enthusiasm for the race ahead. I remembered the gun going off, the sprint to get to the front, and then the dreaded hill. As I recalled the race I suddenly realized something. The person who eventually won never stopped running. Although he was running very slowly and at times seemed to be almost running on the spot, he was going slightly faster than all the others. By the time he reached the top of the hill he was about two or three meters ahead of everyone else. "That's how he won." I thought to myself, "If he could do that, so can I." I replayed the race again in my mind, but this time I imagined it was me who never stopped running. I got in touch with how it would feel to win—and it felt great. Over and over again, I replayed the race with me winning. That night I went to sleep with a deep sense of joy.

As the race approached the next year, I began to remember my imagined winning. This year, I decided that when the race began and I reached the hill, no matter how slow I went, I would not stop running. The day of the race arrived and I just kept imagining myself winning. I said to myself, "You won it last year; you can do it again this year!" As I lined up on the starting line, I renewed my resolve to not stop running. The gun went off and instead of sprinting to the front like the year before, I just started gently running. When the hill arrived I carried on gently running. Many runners were ahead of me, but as I continued up the hill, one by one I passed them. By the time I reached the top, I was in first place. At that moment, I knew in my heart that I was going to win. As the race progressed and no one came to pass me, I felt increasingly filled with bliss. When I arrived at the finish line in first place, I was ecstatic. It was the first race I had ever won. That day I realized the power of imagination. Although I hadn't actually won the race the first year, by deeply imagining that I had, my imagination became reality.

When you rewrite your past you open up a connection to new possibilities and a brighter future. When you feel good, every cell of your body is activated with that feeling. It is your magnet of attraction. If you are one of those people who suffers from hay fever, imagine yourself having a different experience. See yourself walking outside on a bright sunny day and breathing in fresh, sweet air. Imagine your eyes are bright and your lungs clear. There are many people in the world who don't get hay fever. Why not choose to be one of them? Tell a new story—one that feels different.

Changing your mind

Be transformed by the renewing of your mind.

ROMANS 12 VERSE 2

Thoughts are created in our most remarkable piece of bio-engineering—our brains. Your brain is the control center for your entire nervous system. Both the brain and nervous system are made up of special cells called neurons that link together to form an information network called a *neural net*. Scientists have known for many years that the brain runs on electricity, but have more recently discovered that it also runs on light. We each have our own unique neural network, an intricate web of billions of connections where information is conveyed via electricity and stored holographically in light. Your thoughts create pathways within your brain; some are permanent and others temporary. When you use the same thought processes repeatedly, the neural pathways for those processes become hard-wired in your brain. When this happens, we can become locked in fixed patterns of behavior.

Think about the journey you take to work. It can become a mundane pattern if you never vary it. However, just as you can one day decide to drive past the river rather than the strip mall, your brain can do the same. You may have always responded to certain situations the same way, but this does not mean that these responses are written in stone. If there are people in your life with whom you regularly find yourself in conflict, even thinking about them can make you anxious. What if you found something positive about them to focus on? Surely this would open up a new pathway of thought and feeling and your anxiety would diminish.

Your brain has the ability to adapt and change from the moment you are born and throughout the rest of your life. Scientists once thought that when you reached adulthood, your brain was fully formed and that no new neurons were made. In the 1990s, however, research showed that the human brain is constantly making thousands of new neurons every day—particularly in a region of the brain called the hippocampus, which is involved in both learning and memory.

The phrase, "You can't teach an old dog new tricks" just isn't true when it comes to humans. Each time you have a new experience, a new neural pathway is created within your brain. If you repeat that experience often enough, this pathway becomes part of your normal way of thinking. When you start to experience deeper levels of happiness and it becomes the primary way that you think, you will naturally see the best in everything.

Scientists have recently discovered that it takes just fourteen days for a new neuron to develop from its birth within a stem cell to becoming active and wired into a learning network. In mature adults, if these new cells are not used, they die, but when a person learns new tasks, these neurons are incorporated into the neural network of the brain and remain active indefinitely. Indeed, learning occurs almost instantaneously, and scientists now believe that our brains stockpile newly developed neurons specifically to allow for the expansion of our experience and the learning of new skills.

This means you have the ability in every moment of every day to change your mind—to choose a new path and change your reality into one that is completely different from what has been before. Nothing is forever hard-wired in our brains, which are *always* open to change. Everyone has changed their minds. Most people do not like the taste of alcohol at first, but later learn to like the taste. You can learn to like or dislike almost anything—from different foods to different emotional responses. Just because you have been taught self-limiting philosophies, such as "You have to work hard and make sacrifices if you want to be successful" and "Miracles never happen," this does not mean that they have to be true. A belief is only a neural pathway that you use over and over again. When you change your mind and learn to think in new and more expansive ways, new beliefs arise.

When I was a stressed-out manager, I believed that the source of my stress was external—the pressure of work, the long hours, and so on. Once I discovered tai chi, I learned to look within, bringing mind and body into harmony by coordinating my movements with my breathing. Every time I did this, I felt a deep sense of relaxation. I realized that I had the power to change how I was feeling regardless of the external challenges in my life. I changed from focusing my attention on all my problems to looking within for solutions.

Our beliefs mold our reality. The Law of Attraction always brings to you things that match your dominant thoughts and feelings, so if you believe that life is a struggle or that good things never happen to you, this will be the reality you attract. Instead, even as you struggle, turn your mind to a positive outlook, and inspire yourself with blissful thoughts such as "Life is fun," "Good things happen to me all the time," and "I have the power to bring about change." Believe that you are the master of your own destiny and that you have the ability to call into your life anything your imagination can create, and it will become your hard-wired way of thinking.

The ability to change your mind is a powerful tool on your path to happiness. I usually only do things that make me feel good, but sometimes a task needs to be done that I don't feel like doing. In this kind of situation, I change my mind. Either I change my mind by no longer viewing what needs to be done as important, and therefore don't do it, or I change my mind so that I see the fun in doing it. Changing your mind is an ability that becomes easier and easier the more you practice it. The ability to successfully adapt to any situation that arises can become hardwired like any other neural pathway. What used to be difficult can become easy, and what would have made you unhappy can thrill you. All it takes is practice.

———

Sue came to see me having recently been diagnosed with an aggressively growing tumor in her breast. "It has gone from nothing to the size of a baseball in three months," she told me. She said that because there was a history of breast cancer in her family, when she turned forty she started giving herself a breast examination every three or so months. Just over three months ago, she had checked herself thoroughly and felt nothing unusual. Then two weeks ago, while taking a shower, she felt a large lump. She had immediately gone to the doctor and, after an examination and biopsy, was told that she had an aggressive form of breast cancer. Her oncologist said it was life-threatening and suggested a course of powerful chemotherapy followed by surgery.

Sue decided to follow the oncologist's advice and came to me to explore what else she could do to give herself the best chance of survival. I suggested we start by looking at how she was feeling. She said that she was angry with her body for getting cancer and very frightened at the prospect of dying and leaving her young children motherless. She had come to terms with the fact that she was going to lose her hair, but was really worried about the many other possible side effects of her treatment. I pointed out that fear, worry, and anger were of no use to her and that we needed to change her mind-set so that she felt only positive emotions. Here's how we achieved it:

We treated Sue as if she was a top athlete, with each chemotherapy treatment representing a race to be run. We put her on a diet rich in essential nutrients, and prior to each chemotherapy treatment, we switched to a *racing diet* of organic brown rice and vegetables to focus her mind and body. I taught her how to visualize and meditate, which she found particularly powerful. She imagined the different parts of her body as various characters. Her immune system was a scientist in a white coat carrying a clip board, her liver was a police traffic controller at a busy intersection, and her kidneys were two engineers in charge of a water purification plant.

On the morning of each *race day* she meditated and then "talked" to her body. She told the scientist that powerful chemicals would soon be entering her body and that he would need to make sure the blood was extra alkaline to balance this. She warned the traffic controller that a special convoy was arriving that needed to be directed straight to the site of her tumor, and she asked the engineers to be ready to filter any residue of the chemotherapy out of her blood and send it to her bladder. She then imagined running the race with boundless energy and coming over the finishing line in first place. By the time she arrived at the hospital, she was always filled with enthusiasm and excitement.

Her course of chemotherapy went particularly well and she suffered no side effects other than a slight feeling of tiredness on the day after her treatment. The chemotherapy contained a dye, so she could tell when it had left her body by observing the color of her urine. She reported that it took twenty-four hours for her kidneys to clear the drugs out of her system. Upon chatting to some of her fellow patients, she discovered this process took everyone else between two and five days. What was most incredible was that at the end of her treatment, there was no trace of the tumor in her breast whatsoever. Her oncologist said he had only expected the chemotherapy to arrest the tumor's growth and slightly shrink it—he had no explanation for how the tumor had completely vanished. Sue said to me that she knew it was "changing her mind" that had been the key.

Turn things on their head

I once treated a man in his mid-forties who came to see me with digestive problems. At night he suffered from gas pains, and as a result was having trouble sleeping. He had tried eating different foods, taking antacids, herbal supplements, and probiotics, but nothing had worked. The solution I offered was to simply turn his eating pattern upside down. I suggested that he eat his normal evening meal for breakfast and his breakfast at night. Within five days he was pain free.

Sometimes the way to solve a problem is to turn things on their head and do the opposite of what you are currently doing or react in the opposite way to how you normally would. This is especially true if no other solution can be found. Doing the opposite always brings you a new perspective. You can easily experience how profound this can be the next time you walk round your local supermarket or park. Try walking in the opposite direction. You will be amazed at all the new things you see. If you find yourself facing the same unpleasant situations repeatedly, try reacting in the opposite way. If you're tired of listening to your best friend talk endlessly about their troubles, the next time you see them begin your conversation by telling them all the good things you have experienced. If you have trouble getting to sleep at night, try moving your bed to the opposite side of the room. If anything in your life feels mundane, turning things on their head can be great fun and take you into new and exciting experiences.

Feeling better all the time

*Dreams pass into the reality of action. From the actions stems
the dream again; and this interdependence produces the
highest form of living.*

ANAIS NIN

A traveling Buddhist monk arrived at a monastery when
the abbot there was nearing the end of his life. He was
offered an audience with the abbot, but was told that he
could only ask him a single question. The monk accepted
the offer and pondered the best question to ask. Having
made his decision, he entered the abbot's room and bowed
respectfully.

"Master," said the monk, "What are the three most important lessons for one who is seeking enlightenment?"
The abbot lay silently for a few moments and then, with
an ever broadening smile, said, "Attention. Attention. Attention." These were indeed wise words. Whatever we give
our attention to becomes our magnet of attraction. If you
practice giving your attention to happiness, you will attract
happy people and enjoyable experiences into your life every day.

The Buddhists also teach about mindfulness. This means
being aware of what you give your attention to. On your
journey toward bliss, always be mindful of what you give

your attention to and how it makes you feel. Often people unconsciously develop habits that take them away from bliss. For instance, many people religiously watch the news or read the newspaper without ever questioning how that news makes them feel. Much of what the media reports is negative and, just as importantly, never a true account of what occurred. By this I mean that news articles must summarize stories and TV often reduces events to a sound bite.

You might read or hear about great suffering or some tragedy, but you rarely hear about the amazing things humans do and achieve when faced with adversity. Countless acts of heroism, bravery, love, and compassion are so often forgotten when our focus is on the suffering of others. For every negative there is always an equal amount of positive to be seen if we open our eyes and minds to see it.

The next time you hear some bad news, why not give your attention to solutions rather than problems? When you hear about lack, imagine abundance. There is actually enough food on our planet to feed everyone, so when you hear about people starving, imagine a world where no one goes hungry. If we give our attention to how we would like the world to be, we will likely witness more solutions and fewer problems in our own lives. When you hear of conflict, focus your mind on resolution; when you hear of illness, focus your mind on health and healing.

So many people in the world have healed themselves of supposedly incurable diseases just by focusing on healing and bliss. Some have sat for many hours watching comedy programs and have laughed themselves back to health. The human body is truly remarkable, and, given the right set of circumstances, has great powers of self-healing and rejuvenation. The body is like an enormous laboratory where thousands of experiments are taking place, but the mind is the scientist. When the mind is focused on bliss, everything in the laboratory begins to run more smoothly.

Have you ever considered how the things you do and the energies you choose to interact with make you feel? If they don't make you feel good, find a way to stop doing them or a new way of doing them that feels better. If you are always in a rush in the morning, why not set your alarm ten minutes earlier and begin your day with five minutes of meditation? If you start your day with stress, you are much more likely to attract unpleasant challenges throughout your day. Start your day in a positive frame of mind and even challenges will be fun to face and easy to overcome.

When you rest, does it actually make you feel better? Sitting in front of the television watching a soap where the characters are forever arguing and being nasty to each other does not make anyone feel good. If you are feeling tired after a hard day's work, why not relax in a warm bath? Add two cups of Epsom salts or sea salt and perhaps a couple of drops of lavender essential oil and have a good soak. Both Epsom salts and sea salt contain high levels of magnesium, which is known to be a great soother and re-laxer. If you are feeling a little down, why not put on some music and dance or watch a comedy show? Start thinking in terms of "what can I do to make myself feel better?"

Changing your feelings

Think about all the different ways in which you can make yourself feel better, and make a list of positive things to do when you feel down. Consider your five senses: sight, touch, smell, taste, and sound. Anything that stimulates one or more of these senses can activate feelings of plea-sure. For example:

- Reading a good book (see)
- Paddling in the sea (feel)
- Smelling a rose (smell)
- Eating delicious food (taste)
- Listening to relaxing music (hear)

Also think in terms of your physical, mental, emotional, and spiritual well-being. Some activities, such as yoga, tai chi, and massage, improve all four of these aspects at the same time. You could:

- Go for a walk (physical)
- Do a crossword puzzle (mental)
- Watch an inspiring movie (emotional)
- Meditate (spiritual)

Think of new experiences that might be fun to try. Make lists of all the different types of cuisine that you have yet to experience, new places to visit, new skills to learn, and leisure activities to try. As you go through life, always be on the lookout for even more new things and add them to your list.

I have a long list of things that I know will make me feel better. Often it is the simplest things that have the greatest power. In the winter, a nice hot drink is soothing and relaxing, especially if you take time out to sit and savor it. Being out in nature never fails to make me feel calm and relaxed, so every day I make sure that I spend some time outside. Watching the changes that unfold with the turning seasons is fascinating. When you spend time out in nature every day, you see so much that most people fail to notice. I am not an avid bird watcher, but last spring I witnessed a robin find a mate, build a nest, and rear four chicks. Just sitting in my garden each day, watching those birds busy at work, was delightful. I was even lucky enough to see one chick take its first flight. It was a simple, yet magical experience that was thrilling to witness.

I love to dance and find nothing better than putting some great sounds on my stereo and having a good boogie. I practice tai chi and meditation, both of which make me feel calmer and clearer in my mind. I enjoy physical exercise, chopping wood, and mowing the lawn. If ever I lose my sense of bliss, rather than waiting for the feeling to pass, I get proactive. I do something that I know will improve how I am feeling.

Each and every day I give my attention to things that inspire blissful feelings. Since I have done this, life has consistently improved and my happiness has become so deep that now it takes something exceptional to rob me of my inner feeling of well-being.

Recasting the news

Here is a simple exercise to shift your attention away from negative news and turn your mind toward positive thoughts. You can apply this exercise to news you hear on TV, read in the newspaper, or something someone tells you. Whenever you hear some news, ask yourself, "How does this make me feel?" If it evokes positive feelings, bask in those feelings. However, if it is in any way negative, use this technique to find a better feeling:

- In your mind, recast the news by telling yourself a story that feels good. Turn negative to positive. For instance, if you hear about a friend who is very ill, think about them making a remarkable recovery. If you hear about war, imagine peace.
- As you recast the news, get in touch with how much better it makes you feel.
- Smile to yourself as you imagine things turning out great.

Congratulations! You have recalibrated your magnet of attraction. Source Energy is now matching your new, improved feeling and very soon new, blissful feeling experiences will come into your life.

Relieving a mild or moderate headache

Having a headache can be an obstacle to clear thinking, but fortunately, your brain has the ability to turn off pain messages. Here's a mind technique that can ease or completely relieve a mild or moderate headache.

This technique is best practiced first with a headache, but can be used to help relieve pain anywhere in the body.

1. Take three relaxing breaths (see page 12).

2. Close your eyes and focus on the pain in your head. Imagine it as a liquid.

3. Give the liquid a shape and color.

4. See yourself standing in front of a kitchen sink holding an empty glass in your hand.

5. Imagine a hole in your forehead and pour the pain liquid into the glass.

6. Look and see how full the glass is. Now imagine emptying the glass down the sink.

7. Wash the glass out.

8. The pain should now be gone or reduced. If it is only reduced, repeat steps 2–7.

Happiness and appreciation

Gratitude is not only the greatest of virtues,
but the parent of all the others.

CICERO

Psychologists Robert Emmons (University of California) and Michael McCullough (University of Miami) have been conducting a long-term research project on gratitude and thankfulness. In one experiment, they asked three groups of people to spend a few moments each day focusing on different feelings. The first group was asked to list five things that gave them a sense of appreciation, the second group listed five things that irritated them, and the third group cited five events that had occurred in the past week. The results showed that "those who kept gratitude journals on a weekly basis exercised more regularly, reported fewer physical symptoms, felt better about their lives as a whole, and were more optimistic about the upcoming week compared to those who recorded hassles or neutral life events" (Emmons & McCullough, 2003—http://psychology.ucdavis.edu/labs/emmons).

If you want to have bliss peptides coursing through your body and illuminating your cells, there is no better way than being in a state of appreciation. Happiness and appreciation go hand in hand, and when we take time to appreciate the many blessings that life brings us, we naturally increase our sense of inner happiness. And there is so much to appreciate. Just your ability to read these words is reason for appreciation. Isn't it wonderful that you have eyes to read these words and a brain to interpret and understand them? The fact that we have access through books to such a wealth and breadth of information is surely another reason for gratitude. There are many people in the world that never get to read a book—how blessed we are that so much knowledge and information is available to us. When you count your blessings, more will inevitably come your way.

One of the most important things to be grateful for is your wonderful mind and body. We now know that people who love and appreciate themselves are healthier and happier. What's more, if they do get ill, they tend to heal much more quickly than those with low self-esteem. That's because your body never works against you. It is always doing the very best it can for you under the circumstances you present it with. When the mind and body go into partnership, miracles of healing and balancing become possible. These kinds of miracles are happening every day in every corner of the planet.

In our modern society, there is a medical phenomenon called *spontaneous remission*. It occurs when the signs and symptoms of an illness disappear for no known reason.

The current medical explanation is that the patient's own mind activates some form of powerful self-healing. Similarly, in what is called the *placebo effect*, a patient is given a chemically inert substance instead of a drug and yet still manifests an improvement or total cessation of symptoms. The current explanation is that because the patient believes that they are taking a real medicine, they get better through this same self-healing using the power of their own mind. Both these phenomena clearly show that our minds and bodies have tremendous powers of self-healing. If you want perfect health, the mind and the imagination must first dream it up. When we are in appreciation of our bodies, all manner of good-feeling bliss peptides and hormones are released, bathing our cells in a sense of love, joy, and beauty.

Why not take a few moments now to sit and feel in appreciation of your body? It has taken you on so many adventures and experiences. No matter what your current state of health, be thankful for everything about your body that is right. Start at the top of your head and begin appreciating what an amazing being you are. You have a brain that is more powerful than the most powerful of computers, with the ability to modify and change with every passing moment. What a wonderful thing it is to have a brain. How much more challenging life would be if we did not have eyes to see and ears to hear. Our senses are how we interpret everything in our environment. To be able to differentiate different colors, textures, sights, and sounds is something to be both in awe and appreciation of.

Why not take a virtual tour of your body in your mind and appreciate every part of you from arms, hands, feet, and legs, to heart, lungs, liver, and kidneys? Each and every part of you is precious and the pinnacle of creation. As you do this, each part that you focus on in will be bathed in bliss peptides. Your body always responds in a positive way to being told that it is valued, loved, and appreciated. When you do this consistently, you unlock your powers of self-healing.

Another thing to be thankful for is the food we eat. When you take a few moments before a meal to sit and be in appreciation of what you are about to eat, the manner and efficiency of how you digest changes dramatically. Your body begins preparing the right chemicals and enzymes in the correct proportion to most efficiently digest that food even before you have taken a mouthful. The next time you have a meal, before you eat, take a moment to sit and be thankful for it. Your food will taste better if you do. Appreciate the sun and soil that made it grow, the farmers who tended and nurtured that growth, and the many people who made it possible for you to have food on your plate. Imagine your body loving your food and digesting it so efficiently that you absorb only its goodness. Indigenous people have known the power of appreciating and blessing food for thousands of years. Why not try it for yourself and see how different it makes you feel?

Once you start looking for things to be grateful for, the list becomes endless. Having a home, family, and friends is such a blessing. Why not tell a loved one just how much you love and appreciate them? This will uplift both of you. An acupuncturist friend of mine had a simple, and often very, effective cure for depression. He told his patients to get up early each morning and watch the sunrise for ten days. He believed that it was impossible to watch the sunrise every morning without soon feeling an overwhelming appreciation for the wonder of creation and for being alive.

Appreciation is a great way to begin practicing happiness. I find so much in nature that fills me with appreciation. The beauty of trees, flowers, and animals is always thrilling to witness. The more things I find to appreciate, the more I appreciate and celebrate being alive. Try it for yourself.

Setting your day

Happiness cannot be travelled to, owned, earned, worn or consumed. Happiness is the spiritual experience of living every minute with love, grace and gratitude.

DENIS WAITLEY

Wouldn't it be nice if you could have days that are filled with fun, joy, and adventure? Life is meant to be fun, and you have the power within you to make it that way every day. All it takes is five minutes at the beginning of each day to plan how you want to feel during that day. Source Energy only matches your dominant feelings, so if you start the day with good feelings and then find even better feelings, the events and encounters you attract will begin to match and soon you will have that perfect day. How you think and feel at the beginning of the day has a strong tendency to set the tone for that day. If you wake up feeling worried, anxious, or stressed, your day is more likely to be flavored with those feelings throughout—unless you do something to change the way you feel.

No matter how I am feeling, one of the first things I do when I get up is spend five minutes setting my day. It is a cornerstone to my happiness practice. I use this technique to ensure that my day is one filled with endlessly enjoyable experiences. Before setting my day, I usually make myself a nice cup of my favorite herbal tea and go outside into my garden to breathe the fresh morning air. These two things never fail to make me feel good. Having already improved how I am feeling, I then spend a minute or two sitting in appreciation of the many wonderful things in my life. I thank the universe for my lovely wife and my wonderful daughters. I sit in appreciation of our beautiful house and garden, of my friends, and anything else that comes to mind. Having done this, I then set my day.

I imagine the day ahead unfolding with the greatest of ease. If I am writing, I imagine the words coming easily. If I am seeing a client, I imagine us both having a great time together. If I am taking a journey, I imagine clear roads all the way. No matter what I am going to do that day, I visualize a perfect day punctuated with perfect moments. Often I add in a surprise or two because I love surprises. It is always thrilling when something wonderful and unexpected comes my way because it reinforces my belief in my own power to attract good things into my life. And do you know what? Pretty much every day goes according to plan and there is invariably a nice surprise. It might be meeting an old friend, a gift arriving unexpectedly, or bright sunshine when rain was forecast—the list is endless.

Setting my day ensures that I am always focused toward looking for opportunities to feel even better than I am currently feeling. This way, should the unexpected occur, I use it as a means for further improving my positive feelings. For instance, if I am traveling by train and I unexpectedly get delayed or miss my connection, I see it as an opportunity. I don't allow it to change the flavor of my day. Instead, I use this new given time as a further chance to focus positively on the rest of my day ahead.

As my day unfolds, whenever I am about to do something new, I briefly remind myself that I am choosing this new experience to expand my feelings of bliss. For instance, today, before writing, I needed to go into town to buy some food supplies. I had already set this part of my day to go well, but as I got into my car, I again imagined the journey being enjoyable. On the way there, I chose where I wanted to park. I imagined as I arrived at my desired parking space, that a car was just pulling out and I drove straight in. When I arrived there, sure enough a car was just pulling out—my visualization had been so strong that in fact two spaces were free. I drove straight in with a smile on my face. Manifesting parking spaces is great fun and takes no more than a focused thought combined with good feelings.

Setting your day is a simple technique that anyone can apply. It can bring swift and dramatic change into your life in the most wonderful and unexpected ways. No matter where you are and how your life is, by taking five minutes every morning to set your day, your life must, and will, improve. Every time you set your day, you are practicing happiness and with practice comes the realization of your dreams.

Setting your day

- Find a quiet place to sit and take three relaxing breaths (see page 12).

- Think about all the positive things in your life. Sit in appreciation of your amazing body, your friends, your home, and anything else in your life that makes you feel good. Really get in touch with those feelings of gratitude.

- Imagine your day unfolding in the very best possible way. Don't hold back—think big. If you can imagine it, you have the power to make anything reality. Whatever you have planned for that day, imagine everything unfolding perfectly.

- Smile to yourself as you visualize having a day filled with consistently improving feelings.

- Now go and enjoy your day.

The more you work with this simple technique, the more your life will change for the better. You might start to notice that people are nicer to you or that you don't seem to attract the conflicts you used to. As you work with this process, you will learn to expand your horizons and dream bigger and better dreams filled with miracles and surprises. Soon you will marvel at your own power to create your life in a way that consistently expands your bliss. We each have the power within us to change everything in our lives for the better. Each day is like a new beginning, a blank sheet of paper on which you write your unfolding destiny. So ask yourself, "How do I really want my day to be?"

Mending your day

Imagination is more important than knowledge. For while knowledge defines all we currently know and understand, imagination points to all we might yet discover and create.

ALBERT EINSTEIN

The Law of Attraction is an unfailing law that consistently works to bring to you experiences and situations that match your feelings. It does not, however, work instantly. This means that what you are experiencing today may be a match for the feelings you had yesterday, last week, or even last month. As you practice happiness, the Law of Attraction will gradually bring you situations and experiences that match. By improving how you feel, your life will consistently get better.

The more consistently you practice setting your day, the more your days will turn out in ways that feel good to you. There may be times, however, when despite setting your day, things do not turn out the way that you wanted—especially early on. The Law of Attraction is matching how you have felt in your past. It may be hard to accept, but nothing comes into our lives uninvited. Everything that happens to us happens as a result of the feelings we have been holding. If things in life are challenging and difficult, change the way you feel about them and they can become empowering and easy.

Life is all about contrast. Without contrast, our days would be boring and meaningless. Part of the reason we enjoy a warm sunny day is because it feels so much better than a cold dreary day, but without wet days we wouldn't appreciate dry days. When what we have attracted into our lives is not what we want, it gives us the contrast to clarify what we do want. So when things don't go according to plan, take a few moments to ponder the desired outcome. If you have had a conversation where you weren't understood, imagine how much better it feels when what you say makes sense to others. If your journey to work is regularly stressful, regularly imagine it being easy and fun, and it will become that way. This might sound too simple, but simple things are the most powerful.

If your day unfolds in a way that doesn't make you feel good despite setting your day, it is invariably due to the fact that somewhere in your past you have been focusing more on what you don't want than what you do want. Even if you spend time setting your day and feeling good about it, if you don't carry those positive feelings throughout your day, things will not turn out the way you planned. Whenever a stressful situation arises, the last thing we want is for that situation to repeat itself in our future. A great way to change how you feel about such things is a process that I call "mending your day."

At night, just before I go to sleep, I spend a few minutes working with this process. First, I sit in appreciation of all the things that went well and all the positive things that happened to me that day. If certain things have gone really well, I recall them in my mind and immerse myself in feelings of joy and satisfaction that the things I had planned unfolded in the way I'd imagined.

Next, I recall anything that didn't turn out quite right and replay it in my mind. I focus only on what happened and not on how it made me feel. I then rewrite the story in my imagination to turn out the way I would have wanted. As I replay the events in a way that feels so much better, I am resetting my mind toward creating positive feelings. I replay this new, improved version of events in my mind several times until all I feel is joy and satisfaction. By going through this process, I ensure that I always go to sleep with a smile on my face. Remember that whatever you think and feel becomes your magnet of attraction, so it is vital that you start and end your day feeling bliss.

At the core of my healing practice is an understanding that mental health comes before physical health. The Chinese say that all illness begins in the mind, and during my twenty years of practice I have found this to be consistently true. Most people come to me with a belief that if they find health, happiness will follow. However, physical health is only a reflection of how we are feeling; so in truth when we find happiness, health always follows. If you can be happy while still manifesting physical symptoms, think how much easier it will be to keep hold of that happiness once those symptoms have disappeared. Likewise, if you can find happiness within life's stresses, even deeper levels of bliss will await you when the stressors finally leave.

Mending your day

Use this technique at the end of the day to make sure that you go to sleep in a positive frame of mind, ensuring that your magnet of attraction remains positive.

- Take three relaxing breaths.
- Think about the day that has just passed.
- Remind yourself of the positive things that happened to you and be thankful and appreciative of those experiences. If you cannot think of anything, recall any positive event from the past.
- Next, recall anything that did not go well, focusing more on what happened than the feelings it evoked in you.

- Now rewrite the event in a way that feels better. Change negative to positive, rewriting the story so it has the kind of outcome that feels good to you.

- Smile to yourself as you imagine things going perfectly.

- You can repeat this process several times if more than one thing did not turn out the way you would have liked.

- Finally say to yourself, "Tomorrow is going to be a great day."

Once you have practiced this process a few times, you will find that when things don't go to plan in your day, rather than waiting until bedtime to fix them, you will immediately go through this simple process to change how you feel. By doing this, you become much more aware of what doesn't make you feel good, and instantly work on improving that feeling. Soon you will find that rather than dwelling on frustration and disappointment, you will consistently focus on positivity and improved outcomes.

In order to achieve a state of perpetual bliss, we need to look at the things that make us unhappy and change them. Mending your day is the most useful way of achieving this and you can have some great fun working with this technique. The sky's the limit when it comes to using our imagination to change our feelings, and when we do, the body always responds to match those new, improved feelings.

The joy journal

Joy is a flower that blooms when you do.
AUTHOR UNKNOWN

Human beings are the most resourceful of creatures. When presented with a problem, they will invariably find a solution. Whether the problem is big or small, if someone has thought about it and imagined solving it, Source Energy will already be maneuvering the Zero Point Field to bring that solution into actuality. I am always on the lookout for inspiring stories that celebrate human achievement because they remind me that we are all problem solvers. One of my favorite sources for these is a paper and website called *Positive News* (www.positivenews.org.uk).

Every story it tells is inspiring. It is filled with articles about people communicating, cooperating, and manifesting solutions to make the world a better place. It reports about bringing clean water to indigenous people, how music and dance is inspiring young people to find fulfillment away from street gangs, and how innovative thinkers are working to create a more sustainable society. The paper celebrates the many people who are tirelessly campaigning for peace and tells of the different ways in which like-minded people are coming together across the globe to make this world a happier and safer place for everyone. Whenever I read it, I am always inspired by the deep level of caring and compassion that exists on our planet.

This paper inspired me to create something that I call my joy journal. It is a book that I fill with my own positive news. I report anything that inspires me in my joy journal—witnessing a beautiful sunset, an act of kindness, or just listening to the birds singing in the morning. Every day I put an entry into my joy journal, which is another way I set my mind toward looking for the best in everything and everyone. I fill it with positive experiences, thoughts, poems, and pictures.

The joy journal is an excellent tool for helping to lift your spirits if you are ever feeling down. On the rare occasions that I don't feel my normal happy self, I page through my joy journal. Recalling the many blissful things that I have witnessed never fails to put me back into a more positive frame of mind.

There are many different ways of creating a joy journal. You can just write in it, cut out pictures from magazines, add photos to remind you of special times, or even create a "Bliss Blog" on the Internet so that everyone who logs on can share in your positivity. The possibilities are endless. The most important thing is that however you create your joy journal, everything about it must always feel good. Taking a few minutes each day to put an entry in your joy journal forms a powerful magnet of attraction for you to draw even more joy into your life.

Often when I first meet a client, they bring along a few notes on a piece of paper with details of their case history, medication, or other information they think might be relevant. When John came to see me, he arrived with a carrier bag filled with notebooks. Each book represented a year of John's life since he had been diagnosed with chronic fatigue syndrome. He had kept a detailed diary of his illness describing in graphic details his worsening symptoms, negative emotions, side effects from drugs, and so on. He had seven of these books.

He told me that he had seen many doctors and all manner of different healers, but that no one had been able to help him. He handed me his notebooks and said, "Read for yourself, it's all there. I think I am a hopeless case." I scanned the notebooks briefly and then told John I agreed that he was currently a hopeless case, but that I intended to give him a lot more than hope.

I shared with him my understanding of the Law of Attraction and showed him how each of these diaries was a magnet of attraction, drawing ever-greater challenges and problems into his life. I suggested that he burn them and start keeping a joy journal. He followed my advice, and when he came back to see me a fortnight later, he was a changed man. He looked lighter and brighter and he said that he had noticed a marked improvement in his symptoms. Over the next six months, he kept his joy journal every day and it formed the most wonderful story of overcoming adversity and finding healing. The last time I spoke to him, he told me that he had taken up hill walking and was training to go trekking in the Himalayas. Joy journals have the power to change lives, activate healing within the body, and bring you new possibilities for the perpetual expansion of your happiness.

Creating a joy journal

- Find a special book and a favorite pen with which to start your journal.

- Put aside a few minutes at the end of each day to reflect and record the positive experiences of that day.

- One of the best ways to start a joy journal is with a page of appreciation. You might like to write something like, "I feel joy and appreciation that ... ," and then start reeling off the many good things in your life.

- Find a picture that inspires you or a photograph of a loved one to use as a bookmark. This way, every time you open your joy journal, you will immediately be delighted with what you see.

- Write joyfully and freely.
- As you go through your day, always be on the lookout for perfect moments—those times that fill you with joy.

Very soon you will have a vast catalogue of your own positive news to inspire you. If ever you feel down, go back and look at your journal. Remember all the good things that the Law of Attraction has brought you and remind yourself that you can continue to attract an endless stream of positive and bliss-filled experiences.

Wouldn't it be nice?

*If we could see the miracle of a single flower clearly,
our whole life would change.*

BUDDHA

Wouldn't it be nice if whenever you were feeling down, you could immediately do something to make yourself feel a whole lot better? If we want to hold on to happiness and consistently manifest solutions into our lives, it is vital that we do not dwell on negative feelings. When you focus on things that don't feel good, you only attract further situations to match that feeling.

We all have the ability to attract positive change, but in order to do so, we have to find ways to connect with happiness whenever a problem arises. As your feelings improve, your perspective improves, and before you know it, change will have come. One of the best ways to do this is to visualize the solutions you want. When your imagination creates new and improved outcomes, the Law of Attraction acts to bring those possibilities into your reality.

Whenever I don't feel right I try to identify what is making me feel that way, then seek out better feelings by playing a game called *Wouldn't it be nice?* To show you the power of this simple technique, I want to share a magical experience that happened to me last summer.

I have a life filled with variety. I love the freedom of not being tied down to the same routine every day. One day I might be writing, another day teaching, and on another seeing clients. Each day is a new adventure with no two days the same. Occasionally, I don't have any paid work. When this happens, I do other things that I enjoy, such as working in the garden or walking in the countryside. Money ebbs and flows in and out of my life, but I usually have more than enough to pay for the things I need.

Last summer, I had a week in which I didn't have any paid work. I looked at all the things I wanted to do that week and several of them required money. I had a workshop I wanted to attend, food shopping to do, and bills to pay. When I added everything up, I needed £250 to meet all these commitments. The problem was I didn't have £250 and could see no way that it would come in. This did not make me feel good.

Knowing that if I held that feeling I would not attract a solution, I decided to immediately start making myself feel better. I began as usual by making myself a cup of tea and going out into the garden. I sat and looked at all the flowers and trees and reminded myself just how lucky I was to have such a beautiful garden. Now that I felt a little bit better, I began to play the *wouldn't it be nice* game.

"Wouldn't it be nice if £250 came into my life within the next two or three days?" I said to myself. "Yes that *would* be nice. And wouldn't it be nice if it came in a really unusual and unexpected way, a way that thrilled me and reinforced my belief in the Law of Attraction. Yes, that *would* be nice too. And wouldn't it be nice that if I had to do any kind of work to realize this money, it didn't feel like work and in fact it took me on a new adventure?"

On and on I went in my imagination, creating a picture of fun and visualizing myself being filled with joy at my own power to manifest change. I had such a great time with this game, and I was feeling so much better afterward that I no longer cared whether the money came in or not.

"What can I do to continue to expand my bliss?" I pondered.

Now, I happen to really enjoy mowing my lawn. I love the meditative state I feel as I walk up and down with the mower, I love seeing the straight lines in the grass, and afterward I always look with pleasure at how neat and tidy the garden is. So I decided I would mow the lawn while continuing to imagine money flowing easily and effortlessly into my life. Our lawn has two sections, and having mowed the first section, I moved onto our top lawn, which has an old beech hedge growing at one end. As I was mowing, something caught my eye. I turned off the mower and looked down at a small brown patch. It appeared to have a rough and unusual surface.

"What's that?" I said to myself. I prodded the grass and felt a hard lump. I pressed around the edge, and, to my amazement, picked out a rough-skinned black ball about the size of a golf ball. It was a black summer truffle. I prodded the grass nearby and found another one. With a sense of excitement welling up inside of me, I called Debbie into the garden and for the next half hour we had great fun down on our hands and knees poking and prodding at the grass and finding more truffles. We were like a pair of kids having so much fun and laughing together. In the end, we had about twenty truffles of assorted sizes.

"Wouldn't it be nice if I could sell these truffles?" I said to myself. "And wouldn't it be nice if I could get a good price for them? Yes, that *would* be nice." We went indoors, turned on my laptop and searched, "Black summer truffles." The only ones I could find were imported from Italy at prices ranging from £300 to £600 a kilogram. I considered what price I should set for my truffles.

In this kind of situation, I always follow my intuition. I felt that because my truffles were local and rare, they should probably be a slightly higher price than imported ones. A figure of £800 a kilogram (80 pence a gram) popped into my head. I knew I would only be able to sell the truffles to high-end establishments, so I looked in our local phone directory for five-star restaurants and hotels.

I found one that was only a few miles from our home, and called, asking to speak to the head chef. As I was waiting for him to come to the phone I said to myself, "Wouldn't it be nice if I didn't have to haggle, but could just sell my truffles for the price I want?" When the head chef came on the phone and I told him what I was selling and my price, he seemed very interested and invited me to bring my truffles along.

I jumped into my car armed with a small basket brimming with truffles. I arrived at the hotel and found the head chef standing outside the kitchen waiting for me. When he saw the truffles, his eyes lit up. He immediately picked out the two biggest truffles saying they were perfect for a special dish he had in mind. We weighed them and they were 90 grams, which came to £72. He asked me to write him an invoice, which I duly did and handed to him. He thanked me and said that I would receive a check in the post in about three week's time. With that, I left and got back into my car.

It was wonderful that I had sold my first truffles, but I wanted to be paid now—not in three weeks. I could, at this point, have started to feel frustrated and disappointed, but I wasn't about to let that happen. On the journey home

I felt appreciation for having sold the truffles and said to myself, "Wouldn't it be nice if I could sell some more, and wouldn't it be nice if from now on everyone paid me cash? Yes, that *would* be nice!"

I arrived home and telephoned another hotel about eight miles from my home. I spoke with the head chef and got back in my car armed with my remaining truffles. When I arrived there, the head chef met me, immediately fell in love with my truffles, and weighed out 125 grams worth, which came to £100. He turned to one of his assistant chefs and said, "Could you go and get Andy £100 out of petty cash?" Inside I did a jump for joy. What's more, as I was waiting for my money, one of the assistant chefs brought over a glossy brochure of all the hotels in their company's chain, pointed out the local ones, and gave me the names of the head chefs.

Over the next two days, I spent my time traveling to visit the very best hotels in my area, talking to chefs who were deeply passionate about their food, and selling my truffles for cash. By the end of the two days, I had £250 in cash and, of course, I had a further £72 due to arrive in three weeks. I was ecstatic and knew without any shadow of a doubt that the Law of Attraction really works. Now whenever I am not feeling my usual happy self or a situation arises that is not to my liking, I play the *wouldn't it be nice* game. It never fails to make me feel better and attract real solutions into my life.

The *"Wouldn't it be nice"* game

Here is a perfect game to play whenever you are feeling down. It will quickly connect you back to your bliss and direct your attention toward attracting positive outcomes.

- Find a quiet place where you won't be disturbed and take three relaxing breaths (see page 12).

- Imagine yourself attracting wonderful solutions to all your current problems. Start to think of what you really want right now and say to yourself, "Wouldn't it be nice if … ," then imagine things the way you would ideally like them to be.

- Really get in touch with the feelings this game evokes. Imagine just how great you are going to feel as you witness solution after solution manifesting in your life.

- Once you have reactivated your bliss, smile to yourself and sit in appreciation of how easy it is to make yourself feel better.

- Go and do something that you enjoy to lock this improved feeling into your consciousness.

Next time life is not quite how you want it to be, why not play this game? If you really immerse yourself in how you want your life to be, the Law of Attraction will bring you unexpected solutions, and you will start to believe and know that your life *can* be filled with magic.

Variety is the spice of life

Your brain works best when it has a steady flow of new input every day. When we repeat the same routines over and over again, they become uninspiring and dull and we literally lose our shine. Finding new ways of doing things, exploring new avenues, and learning new skills makes sure your mind is clear and sharp. Routines can be useful, but changing your routines regularly means that you will always generate new and interesting experiences. Why not read a book on a subject that is completely outside of your normal range of interest? If you love opera, go to a pop concert for a change. If you always watch football, why not go to a basketball game? Do you remember the wonder of all the endless stream of new experiences you had when you were a child? For most people, childhood is an endless adventure of learning, but that adventure does not have to stop when you grow up. Having lots of variety in what you do and see will help to keep you fresh and feeling younger.

Every day is a holiday

*Celebrate the happiness that friends are always giving, make
every day a holiday and celebrate just living.*

AMANDA BRADLEY

Holidays are wonderful times to practice making the best
of every situation. When we are on holiday (vacation) we
tend to be in a completely different frame of mind than
when we are doing our day-to-day work. We have an attitude toward enjoying ourselves because we know the time
is short. When we go on holiday, even if it is raining, we
don't let the weather dampen our spirits. We might have
been planning a nice day down at the beach, but if it rains
we invariably make the best of things by finding something
else to do. Perhaps we might go to a movie, see a show, or
have a long lunch.

We all have the ability to make the best of the situations
we find ourselves in, but many people only use this ability when they are taking a holiday. You can, if you choose,
have this attitude every day. Why not treat every day as if
you were on holiday? Make every day special. When events
take an unexpected turn, especially if they prevent you
from doing something fun, make the most of the situation and find the next best alternative that feels good. If
you knew that today was going to be your last day on this

planet, wouldn't you savor each and every experience no matter how mundane it might normally seem? You can experience precious moments all the time—any day, every day.

When we are on holiday, we worry less and enjoy more. We also tend to be far more "in the moment," rather than being concerned about the past or the future. If you can feel happy in the present, the future will bring you more happiness. If you are always open to change, you will be able to adapt and navigate through even the most unexpected twists with ease. Having positive thoughts and feelings brings about the consistent production of bliss peptides that carry you through each new experience with a sense of fun and enjoyment.

Make the very best of everything that happens to you. Each experience is just a moment in time; so be in the moment and make it fun. Have eagerness and excitement for all that unfolds in your life and appreciation of those simple things that lift your spirits. When you wake up, think to yourself, "Isn't it wonderful that I can sleep? Isn't it a blessing to have a bed to sleep on and a roof over my head?" As you use the bathroom, show appreciation for the people who invented plumbing and toilet paper. How much harder life would be for us if we didn't have running water. Whatever the weather, be thankful that it is here.

How wonderful it is that we do have rainy days to feed the plants and trees, and the streams and rivers.

Prime yourself to make the very best of every moment. Tap into your unlimited resourcefulness so that you easily adjust to unexpected situations. Above all, have fun. Treat every day as an adventure, and be ready to be surprised at the wonder and magic of this amazing world we live in. If you paint every day with bright colors and blissful feelings, your future will always be bright.

My dream vacation

Think about your dream vacation and write down all the things you would like to experience during that vacation. For instance you might write:

I want to experience:

- Warmth and sunshine
- Meeting new people
- Going to new places
- Eating different foods

Write down as many different things as you can think of, making sure that everything you write inspires positive feelings. Read through your list and spend a few minutes imagining how wonderful your vacation feels. Now look and see how many of these experiences you can bring into your everyday life. For instance:

- Warmth and sunshine—on warm sunny days, take a few minutes to go outside and enjoy the feeling of the sun on your skin. If you like your holidays really hot, why not book into a sauna or steam room and spend your time there imagining your dream holiday? If it is cold and dull outside, make yourself a hot drink, and with your eyes closed, imagine bathing in warm sunshine as you drink it.

- Meet new people—why not go to a new class or join a club? Many leisure classes and clubs offer introductory "taster" sessions so you could try several different things and meet lots of new people.

- Go to new places—Get a map of your local area and find places that you haven't visited before. Visit art galleries, churches, parks, local landmarks, and interesting buildings. You will be amazed at how many new places you can experience so close to home.

- Eating different foods—Find restaurants in your local area that specialize in foods you haven't tried before or go to your library and find a cookbook and make your own new dishes.

The more things you can experience in the here and now that are similar to your dream holiday, the stronger your magnet of attraction will be. Feel those feelings and the Law of Attraction will bring your dream to you. While you are waiting, you will be inspiring yourself with a whole host of new and exciting things.

Practice makes perfect

Practice is the best of all instructors.

PUBLILIUS SYRUS

In the early 1990s, psychologist K. Anders Ericsson and two colleagues at Berlin's Academy of Music began a study to access the link between talent and achievement (www .psy.fsu.edu/faculty/ericsson.dp.html). They divided violin students into three groups. The first group was made up of child prodigies who were expected to become world-class soloists. The second group consisted of students who were considered "good," having the ability to become professional musicians playing in orchestras. The third group consisted of "average" students who were not expected to become professional musicians, but who intended to be music teachers in schools.

At the age of twenty, all students were asked the same question, "Over the course of your entire career, how many hours have you practiced?" The results were surprising. Every member of the study started playing at roughly the same age, around five years old. By the age of eight, only those students who practiced the most ended up being the highest achievers in their class, regardless of ability. The elite performers were all practicing in excess of thirty hours a week by the age of twenty and had already totaled more than ten thousand hours of practice throughout their lives. By contrast, those who became orchestral musicians had logged only eight thousand hours, and those who became music teachers, only four thousand.

Ericsson and his colleagues then looked at pianists and found the same results. What was particularly striking in both studies was the fact that no child prodigies became elite performers if they practiced less than their peers. Similarly, no one who worked extra hard failed to break into the top ranks. All the highest achievers were those who practiced the most. Furthermore, reaching the highest level appeared to always take roughly ten thousand hours of practice. All the current studies of high achievers, including musicians, sportsmen, writers, chess players, and even master criminals, show the same result—it takes ten thousand hours of practice to become a world-class expert in anything.

———

When you become an expert in Blissology, you will be living the life of your dreams. You will be so filled with happiness, that the Law of Attraction will bring you an unending supply of everything you desire. Based on the above research, you'll need to practice ten thousand hours.

The wonderful thing is that you can practice Blissology all day, every day just by always looking for better feelings. Let's say you are awake fourteen hours a day. This means that with two years of consistent practice, you can potentially realize all of your dreams.

We have seen how making new neural connections opens us up to new experiences and possibilities. It is possible for you to experience happiness all day, every day. Remember, there is no limit to how good you can feel. Imagine experiencing life as a forever-expanding adventure filled with a forever-expanding sense of happiness. Wouldn't that be nice? Being happy can become a habit if you regularly and consistently activate the neural pathways that connect you with that feeling.

By practicing the exercises I have shared with you, you can become a master of happiness. Happiness can become the way you naturally feel, hard-wired in your neural net. No matter how happy you are currently feeling, there is always a better feeling that you can seek out. When you consistently work to improve how you feel, your sense of inner well-being, increased self-esteem, and the connection to your inner wisdom becomes ever stronger. Our brains become hard-wired to habitually choose happiness—to seek out new thoughts and to dream new dreams.

When you are happy, you increase the amount of light that is active within your body. You shine brighter, and in doing so, you illuminate the wisdom that is held within each of your cells. In the quantum world, particles such as the photons of light do not always exist as distinct objects. All quantum particles have two states of being, one as a wave and the other as a particle. These two states of being have very different properties. A wave is like a field of possibilities, and when light exists as a wave, the photons of light within that wave have an unlimited number of potential positions. A particle comes into existence only when the unlimited possibilities of a wave collapse into one position.

Quantum experiments indicate that when you study light indirectly, it behaves like a wave of possibilities, but when you study it directly, those possibilities collapse into one single reality. While physicists are still debating whether or not all these potential possibilities exist simultaneously in unlimited parallel universes, we can experience our reality as only one distinct set of possibilities collapsing into a single unfolding event—at a time, that is.

The key to bringing all the possibilities of the quantum world into form is consciousness. Just as scientists do not conduct random experiments to try to understand naturally occurring phenomena—they consciously start with a hypothesis to test discrete portions of it—it is our consciousness that forms the very fabric of our reality. Consequently, when you change your consciousness, you change your experience of reality.

When you practice consistently giving your undivided attention to what you want in your life, it must come to you. When you conscientiously work to improve how you are feeling, happiness becomes your day-to-day experience. Do not wait for life to change for the better before you feel better. Improve how you feel and life will always change to match those new feelings. It is possible to live the life of your dreams and have new and wonderful experiences every day. Every time you practice a technique to improve how you are feeling, you are reaffirming the belief that happiness is your destiny. You are rewiring your neural net and reaffirming your new positivity.

Remember, practice can sometimes be challenging—any time you learn new skills it takes a while for you to perfect them. For instance, when learning to drive a car, there are so many different things to think about. You have to watch where you are going while also checking your mirrors and working the pedals. At first it seems like you'll never remember it all. But after steady and consistent practice, the individual components needed to drive well become second nature. They become so natural that you can hold an intense and deep conversation with someone while driving perfectly. As you practice being happy, it too will become your natural way of being. You will forget about needing to make yourself feel better because you will naturally be doing it all the time in every situation. Happiness will have become your true, blissful nature.

Set your mind to bringing that sense of enjoyment into your life every day. Wake up every morning with the expectation of having a great day. Set your day in a way that feels really good to you. Let your imagination flavor each day with sweetness and light. Dare to believe in miracles and the arrival of wonderful surprises. Open your mind to a lighter and brighter way of being.

As you go through your day, enjoy the contrast that life brings you. When blissful feeling experiences come into your life, sit in appreciation of your ability to create a beautiful reality. When things happen that don't make you feel good, get proactive and do something to make yourself feel better. Set your mind to a better way of feeling and the Law of Attraction will make it so.

Living Happiness

Broadening your horizons

Success is not the key to happiness. Happiness is the key to success. If you love what you are doing, you will be successful.

ALBERT SCHWEITZER

When you consistently work on increasing your happiness, the things that you attract into your life will begin to match those new, improved feelings. Life will start to become easier and much more fun. Problems that have persisted for a long time will suddenly resolve themselves, and where you experienced conflict, you will start to see peace. As you become happier, your world expands. New possibilities start to show themselves broadening your horizons and improving your quality of life. Soon you will have a life that is filled with blissful experiences, and things you only dreamed about will start to become real possibilities. Wouldn't it be nice to have the life of your dreams? You can have anything that your heart desires; your dream home, perfect health, great relationships, and financial abundance. If you can imagine it and feel it, you can manifest it.

Every successful person uses the Law of Attraction either consciously or subconsciously. Some of them are happy, but others are clearly not. So what is the key to being both successful and happy? The key lies in following your heart. Let us leave the world of science for a moment and step into the metaphysical. A different perspective will bring new insights that can help you to realize the life of our dreams *and* be happy at the same time.

There are two broad ways in which people interact with the world around them. There are people who are *self-centered* and those who are *heart-centered*. We all have an ego for a reason—it is our own uniqueness. The ego gives our personality its flavor. However, if our egos become the dominant factor in our lives, we tend to be self-centered. Our desires revolve around alleviating the negative feelings we hold within us rather than transmuting those negative feelings into positive ones. This makes our magnet of attraction one that might bring us some success, but not happiness.

When the ego is dominant, we seek to exert our will upon the universe and those around us. Our primary motivation is to relieve our negative feelings rather than to cultivate positive ones. However, when the heart is open we create a reality that feels very different. We begin to understand that in order to change the world, we must first change ourselves. We become motivated by a desire to consistently feel better and to make the world a better place. An open heart is the key to being successful *and* happy.

The heart-centered person has a worldview that embraces the idea that everyone can find happiness. If they desire to be rich it is because they recognize how being rich can broaden their horizons and create the possibility for them to share their happiness with the world. Rich people who are heart-centered tend to use their money to improve the quality of other people's lives as well as their own. They do not look to the world, other people, or circumstance to bring them happiness. They connect with bliss for themselves and by themselves, and then share those good feelings with others. Success comes to them easily because it is a byproduct of their happiness. Only when you open your heart can true happiness come into your life. This requires your ego to surrender its position of dominance and for the deeper and more spiritual part of your being, your higher-self, to become your guiding light.

Your higher-self is your connection to Source Energy. It knows the quickest and best-feeling way to bring all your heart's desires to you. When you follow your feelings and listen to your intuition, you are listening to your higher-self. With an open heart, every experience becomes an opportunity for personal growth and improving how you are feeling. Some people advise that we listen to our heads rather than our hearts, but to do so means to ignore how we are feeling. In fact, how we are feeling is the most important aspect of our lives here on Earth. The quality of your life is not dictated by what you do—it's how you feel about your activities that matters.

When you open up your heart, you open yourself up to an expansive and broader view. You are no longer limited by your beliefs, and you begin to understand that miracles and magic are possible. Opening your heart opens a doorway into the abundance of a forever-expanding universe. What the universe can supply is limitless because it is formed by the dreams and desires of your forever-expanding consciousness.

One of the first things I do with all my clients is to get them in touch with their feelings. It is without doubt the quickest way to bring change into your life. When you start to improve how you feel and dream of a better life, change happens. When Karen came to see me, she was recovering from the first of two surgeries. After a motorbike accident she had damaged her jaw and teeth. The first surgery was relatively minor and had involved the removal of several teeth that were damaged beyond repair. She then had to wait two weeks for the swelling to go down before having a second operation: major surgery that involved resetting her damaged jaw.

When I spoke to Karen, she was very worried about her forthcoming operation. She had found the previous minor surgery very stressful. The surgeon she met seemed preoccupied with going to the theater that evening and did not really explain any of the procedure. This left her confused and frightened. The nurse assigned to Karen was cold and unsympathetic, and the anesthetist hardly said two words to her. No one did anything to allay her fears.

When she woke up after surgery, although relieved that she was okay, she could not get the next surgery out of her mind. It filled her with dread, which is why she came to see me. We only had ten days before her next operation, so the only work we did together was to focus Karen on filling her days with things that evoked good feelings. She spent time with friends, rested whenever she felt tired, only watched television programs that she enjoyed, and practiced a few simple mind exercises.

We met again on the day before her operation and she was in a much more positive frame of mind. I took her through a visualization of her surgery, imagining everything she experienced feeling good. We opened her mind to the possibility of having a new and positive experience. What Karen experienced the next day was an almost polar opposite of her previous operation. The surgeon spent nearly an hour with her before her operation explaining exactly what was going to happen and clearly answering all her questions. The nurse assigned to her was caring, gentle, and kind, and the anesthetist was so reassuring and communicative she felt complete trust in him. The surgery was a complete success and her recovery was unusually fast. The Law of Attraction brought Karen a new experience that matched her new, improved feelings.

To become a master of Blissology requires you to let love guide you. When you love yourself unconditionally, you naturally connect with the beauty that is really you. Follow your dreams out of a love for yourself and you will not only find happiness, but will have it in such abundance that it will spill over onto everyone you meet.

As you focus on the life of your dreams, be sure that you are motivated only by a desire to experience better feelings. Do not look for the realization of your dreams to mask the pain of your past. Know that you can heal anything by consistently following your bliss. We have explored the possibility of you living the life of your dreams and having days filled with adventures. Happiness is the precursor to all of this. So, having made ourselves feel better, let us step into the art of happiness and dream about how you really want your life to be.

Daring to dream

Every great dream begins with a dreamer. Always remember,
you have within you the strength, the patience, and the
passion to reach for the stars to change the world.

HARRIET TUBMAN

Wouldn't it be nice if you could imagine something your heart desires and then have it arrive at your feet with ease? At some point, most people fantasize about the things they would really like to come into their lives. Whether it is a new job, a great relationship, or a dream holiday, it always feels nice to let our imaginations fly. What many people do not realize is that if they remained focused only on what feels good, that dream would very quickly become real. The reason most people don't get what they really want is because they either focus more on what they don't want, or the fundamental energy behind what they want—the reason why they want it—is not correct.

If you imagine your perfect job, but afterwards say to yourself, "That will never happen to me because my life's not like that," you have negated your magnet of positive attraction. If you want that dream holiday in order to temporarily escape from the frustration and unhappiness of your life, your magnet of attraction is not the holiday, but the frustration and unhappiness. What is the point in dreaming of being rich if your motivation is only to allevi-ate your fear of poverty? When this is the case, the fun-damental energy behind what you want is fear—and fear becomes your magnet of attraction.

Whenever I see a client, whether for a health problem, emotional issue, or business problem, the first question I always ask them is "What do you want?" People tend to focus too much on their problems, but I have found that life becomes much more easy and fun if you focus on solu-tions. If you know what you want, you have a clear direc-tion to head toward. So ask yourself the question, "What do I want?" Think about how you would really like your life to be. Let your motivation be only to improve your overall sense of well-being; in other words, to feel better. Focus only on what feels good.

There are so many things you can imagine feeling good about. You can have anything your heart desires, so let's dare to dream a little. What about imagining your dream life? What kind of house would you like to live in? What kind of car would you like to drive? What kind of relation-ships would you like to have? What kind of work would you like to do? Think hard and deep about these things and begin to paint a picture in your mind of your perfect life. Do not be afraid to think big. Don't let your beliefs limit your imagining. Most of all, do not worry about how these things could become real—just have fun dreaming.

Have you ever moved into a new house? A new house is a blank canvas on which you can paint your personality. No matter what your previous home was like, a new house signals an opportunity for change. You can start fresh and paint a new picture of your life. If you have moved from a smaller home into a larger one, there is a sense of appreciation of the new space you have. You marvel at having more rooms or a bigger garden. What fun it is when we go through transitions that improve our quality of living.

What is your ideal house? How many bedrooms would you like? What size garden feels best? Would you like it to be in the city or the country? What about a swimming pool? Imagine the kind of home that you would ideally like to live in. Don't think about how much this home might cost or how you need to change your life in order to make it possible—just focus on positive feelings. If you had unlimited funds, what kind of house would you buy? Try to get a clear picture of it in your mind and imagine yourself standing outside with the keys in your hand and a big smile on your face.

Taking ownership of a brand new car feels great. When you get into it, it is clean with that fresh, new-car smell.

Everything about it feels new and exciting. As you learn to drive it, you open new neural pathways of learning. At first it might seem awkward to drive in an unfamiliar car, but as those neural pathways become more frequently used, the experience becomes easier. Soon the car feels like yours, and you are totally comfortable driving it.

You experience a whole new adventure when you first get into a brand new car. It marks the beginning of fresh adventures to new places and experiences. If you could choose any car, what kind of car would you like to drive? Perhaps there is more than one car you would like to drive. That's fine. This is *your* dream, so dream it the way that feels best to you. Close your eyes and see yourself behind the wheel, smiling and feeling great. Imagine the sense of appreciation you feel as you drive it back to your dream home for the first time.

Sharing love with someone special is one of the deep joys of being human. Being in love feels great. When you are in a relationship where there is love, understanding, and compassion between both parties, it is a true pleasure. It is great to have a playmate in life, someone who understands you, who knows the kinds of things that you enjoy. You can have a beautiful and happy relationship if you dream your life that way. What kind of relationship would you really like? If you could create your dream partner, what picture would you paint? It is always blissful to love and be loved. Imagine the two of you having the best fun in the world and sharing wonderful adventures in exotic places. Paint it in your mind the way you would really like it to be. Paint a picture that feels really good to you.

There are no limits to the wonderful things you can attract into your life. We live in an abundant universe that expands in tune with our desires. There is plenty to go around, so don't be afraid to dream big. Remember, if you can imagine it, you can attract it. I have seen so many people change their lives by learning to expand their dreams.

Jo was a model who came to see me with work-related stress. She modeled for catalogs and often worked six days a week. She was paid fairly well, but found the hours very long and demanding. When I asked her to focus on her ideal life, she told me she dreamed of being a top model, being paid more but working less.

Having identified her dream job, I explained to Jo that in order to attract it into her life, she needed to live happiness now. We began working on Jo feeling better about her current work. We focused on all the positive aspects about her work, and reminded her of the fun and enthusiasm she experienced when she first worked as a model. We also made her one day off each week a special day. Jo would fill this day with fun-filled activities. Two months later, she was approached by one of the top fashion labels to be the face of their new fragrance for the next three years. They asked to her sign an exclusive contract requiring her to do only three five-day shoots a year. The money they offered was four times her current salary. This job was even better than she had imagined.

———

John came to see me with chronic back pain caused by his work as a gardener. He loved working outdoors, but found the endless digging and weeding very hard. I gave him acupuncture to ease his back pain, and we talked about the kind of work he would really like to do. John said that he still wanted to work outdoors, but had no real idea of what his dream job would be. Instead of focusing on a specific job, I asked John to think of his ideal working environment. He said that he wanted to work in the countryside, preferably with trees, meet lots of different people, and do something to take care of nature. I treated John over several weeks, and each acupuncture treatment helped him feel better. While he was having his treatments, I asked John to focus his mind on his dream working environment.

A short while later, he met an old school friend who he had not seen for twenty-five years. As they shared stories from their lives, his friend suddenly said, "I know about the perfect job for you." He told him about a vacancy with the Forestry Commission that met all the requirements for his ideal job. John applied, and a month later was living his dream. Prior to meeting this old friend, he had no idea how he would find his dream job. Fortunately, Source Energy knew exactly how.

———

Everything in life starts as a thought. That thought is a magnetic vibration that we send out into the universe. By the Law of Attraction, a thought will attract similarly vibrating thoughts until it becomes a collection of thoughts, called a *thought-form*. A thought-form has a stronger, more coherent attractive force than a single thought, and it draws to itself similar thought-forms. As the Law of Attraction brings all these similar thought-forms together, that original thought is transformed from being a possibility into a probability, and finally into a certainty. Excitement, enthusiasm, and joy take center stage to guide you on your way. So if you want to live the life of your dreams, you have to first think it into being. Take some time now to think about everything you would like to experience in your life from this moment on.

Fixing your dream

The moment one definitely commits oneself, then Providence moves too. All sorts of things occur to help one that would never otherwise have occurred. A whole stream of events issues from the decision. Raising in one's favor all manner of unforeseen incidents and meetings and material assistance which no man could have dreamed would have come his way…

GOETHE

Have you noticed that children today seem to have been born with the knowledge of how to use technology? I see three-year-olds using a computer mouse as naturally as if they had always done so. How does this happen? The dreams and aspirations of one generation are often lived out in the next one. When lots of people have the same thought, by the Law of Attraction it must sooner or later become real. How many people, when they were first learning to use a computer, wished it could be easier to master? These collective thoughts go out into the universe and Source Energy always matches their vibration. However, because most people don't bring themselves into alignment with their desires, it takes the next generation to manifest them. Bringing yourself into alignment with Source Energy means raising your feelings of bliss to the same level they would be if your dream came true. If you can feel this good about your dreams the moment you start dreaming, they will come true all the quicker.

When you open your mind and dare to dream of a wonderful life, just the process of dreaming makes you feel better. Each heart's desire becomes a powerful magnet of attraction. When you dream of a life filled with bliss-ful experiences, the universe expands with those new pos-sibilities, and Source Energy moves to bring that vision in actuality. If you commit to happiness, the life of your dreams will come to you effortlessly. The more you dream, the better you will feel, and the better you feel, the more you will dream. Our every wish and desire is held as a pos-sibility within Source Energy—like prizes waiting for us to claim them.

For your dreams to become real, you need only do two things. First, you must dream the dream, and second, bring yourself into alignment with it. When you are living the life of your dreams, you are living happiness. Therefore, for you to come into alignment with your dreams, you have only to bring yourself closer and closer to that feeling of bliss. When you live happiness, there is nothing that you cannot do and no dream that you cannot make real.

How your dreams become real is not your work—that is the work of Source Energy. You can only think of "how" based on your experiences from the past. When you focus on the how, you negate the possibility of the unexpected or extraordinary from coming into your life. Source Energy knows the best way to bring your dreams to you, and if you trust in your own ability to attract change, the how will reveal itself one step at a time. Your work is to follow your good feelings and feel your way to bliss. For when you do arrive at bliss, you will find that all your dreams will meet you there.

The quickest, most efficient way to call your dreams toward you is to focus only on things that inspire happiness. If you do *only* what feels good, you will manifest solutions and your heart's desires very, very quickly. Many people believe that their dreams will only come true if they put in the hard work. Hard work, whether mental or physical, should only be part of your unfolding dream if it makes you feel good.

Once you have decided the things you want to call into your life and the kinds of experiences you want to have, the best way to fix that dream is to fine-tune it. The more specific you are, the easier it is for Source Energy to bring *exactly* what you desire.

———

Fifteen years ago, Debbie and I decided that we wanted to move from our house in London into the countryside. We made a wish list of everything we wanted for our new house. I had dreamt of living in an old house with thick stone walls and a big garden. I visited such a house in my childhood and fell in love with its rustic charm. Debbie loved old houses too, so we started our dream with "An old stone house in the countryside with a big garden." We wrote down how many bedrooms we wanted, what size garden, the things we wanted nearby, and so on. We fine-tuned our vision by writing everything we could possibly think of for our dream house. When we had finished, we had filled a large piece of paper. We then read through all we had written to further fix the vision in our minds.

I contacted real estate agents telling them broad details of what we wanted. The following morning, a large bunch of property details came through the mail. I remember opening the first envelope and looking briefly at the photos of the various properties on the front of each of the details. I looked at the first one and immediately thought, "No, that's not the right one." I did the same with the next four properties. When I looked at the fifth property, I immediately knew that this was the house of our dreams. I showed it to Debbie, and she felt the same.

Later that week we went to view the house. It ticked every single one of the items on our wish list. We had all manner of obstacles and challenges to overcome to actually buy our house, but we found solutions to all of them. Every day we spent five minutes focusing on our dream and imagining ourselves living in our new home. Throughout the day, we kept talking excitedly about it. Two people focusing on the same dream makes for an even more powerful magnet of attraction.

The day we moved in, Debbie and I were thrilled and amazed at our power to manifest the house of our dreams. A few weeks later, my parents came to visit. They loved the house, too. I reminded them of the old house we had visited when I was a boy and told them how, since then, I had dreamt of living in a big house with thick stone walls and a big garden. They remembered the visit, but informed me that it was actually just a little cottage. It did have thick stone walls, but only half the size of the ones we had in our new home. It had a garden, but again it was half the size of our new one. As a small boy, the house and garden had seemed very big. As I had grown up, I had kept that image in my mind and translated the sizes up subconsciously. My dream had grown with me.

As you think about all the wonderful things you would like to come into your life, be as specific as possible. For instance, if you want a new car, ask yourself what make, model, and color feels best to you? What kind of interior would you like? Do this for every one of your desires. Imagine feeling that sense of excitement as you expect them and the thrill when they arrive. The more you can play this game and feel those positive feelings, the stronger your magnet of attraction will be. All sorts of wonderful events and connections take place once we firmly commit to something, so why not commit to your dreams? The world is your oyster, and there are unlimited pearls for you to discover. Think big, think fun, and let your imagination fly.

Holding your dream

Dream lofty dreams, and as you dream, so you shall become.
Your vision is the promise of what you shall one day be; your
ideal is the prophecy of what you shall at last unveil.

JAMES ALLEN

The art of living happiness is not just about dreaming of a
happier life, but becoming the perpetual artist of your life.
Once you have formulated your dream life in your mind
and fixed it by fine-tuning as many specifics as possible, you
can help to hold that dream in your consciousness by further activating your powers of imagination and creativity.

When interior designers design a room, they first create
a vision of it in their mind. As a new idea is forming, they
will then fine-tune it in a manner similar to how I suggest
you fix your dreams. Once this is done, they often create
a design book. They fill it with samples of the kinds of
things they want in the room. It might be a piece of col-
ored card that matches the main color they want, pictures
of the furniture they would like, and so on. This process
helps them clarify every aspect of their dream. If at any
time they lose sight of their vision or they feel any confusion about what they really want, they simply refer back
to their design book. Many artists and creative people use
this kind of tool to help them manifest what they have

envisioned in their minds. You can do the same for your dream life.

Designing your future can be as easy as extending the idea behind the joy journal (see page 76), which involves creating a diary of all the good things that have happened to you so that you can always see the positive aspects of your past. Why not create a dream book filled with the blissful things you want to happen to you in the future? Create a page called, "My Dream Car," another one called "My Dream House," and so on. Look in magazines for pictures that help to remind you of that dream. For your dream house, you can cut out pictures of similar looking houses, the kind of furniture you want, the views you would like, and so on. If you would like to live by the sea, create a collage of images connected with the sea, and place a picture of the kind of house you want in the middle of it. The more creative you are, the more powerful your magnet of attraction will be.

Making your own dream book

Here is a wonderful way to help you hold and expand your dreams so that you are continually adding new color and imagination to the things you desire in your life. You are the designer and artist of your own life, so craft this book in a way that feels good to you.

- Find a blank, large-format book, such as a leather-bound notebook, a scrapbook, or an A4 pad.

- On the opening page, write an appropriate title, such as "My Book of Dreams."

- Find a photograph of yourself looking happy and relaxed and stick it on the first double page.

- Around the outside of this photo, write titles of the many things you dream of attracting into your life. These can include such things as, "My Dream Home," "My Dream Car," "My Dream Job," and "My Dream Relationship."

- On the next double page, choose the title that is most important to you and write it in the centre of the page.

- On the following pages do the same for each of your dream titles.

- As you journey through life, be on the lookout for anything that resonates with your dreams. If you see a picture or a color that fits into one of your dreams, cut it out and stick it in your dream book on the page with the appropriate dream.

- Very soon you will have a book filled with inspiring pictures, thoughts, and ideas. These will help you clarify every aspect of your many dreams. Let your

imagination flow and craft your book of dreams
in ways that fill you with feelings of excitement,
anticipation, and a forever expanding vision for
your future.

Different people find different ways to hold their dream.
Some create dream books like I have suggested above while
others create vision boards on which they place reminders
of what they would like to come into their lives. Some people write affirmations, such as "Money comes into my life
with ease," or "Every day I am blessed with healing," on
Post-it notes and stick them in prominent places at home,
in their cars, or at work. All these tools act as constant reminders of the wonderful things you want to call into your
life so that your magnet of attraction remains strong.

The power of dream books and vision boards is really
in how they make you feel. They should always make you
smile whenever you see them. They act as a reminder that
you are always the creator and artist of your own life. You
and you alone decide what kind of experiences you want
to have. When you consistently improve the way you feel
about yourself and about the possibilities of your future,
your life must change for the better. The Law of Attraction
does not pick and choose who it works for. It works with
everyone, every moment of every day.

If you forget your vision or lose sight of your dreams, referring to your dream book will remind you that you are the wonderful creator of your own reality, and there is nothing that cannot be yours. Don't forget that it is not your work to focus on the *how* of your dreams—that is the work of Source Energy. Your work is only to dream and follow your bliss.

How to clear bad feelings

If someone upsets you or if you still feel negative emotion toward someone in your past, here is a great way to clear those feelings from your mind. Write the person a letter saying exactly how you feel. You are not going to send this letter and no one else will read it, so you can say anything and everything. Use whatever language you want. Express all your anger, hurt, pain, and other negative feelings— speak your mind. Once you have written all you can, re-read the letter. If it brings up more emotion, write that down too. Read the letter one final time and then immediately burn it. This sets a clear intent that you want these negative feelings out of you.

Now write a simple letter of forgiveness and then burn that, too. Forgiveness is very important for healing from the hurt others have caused you. Forgiving does not mean you are condoning their actions, it really means that you forgive yourself for attracting it. The forgiving letter sets a clear intent that you no longer want the person in your letter to have any kind of negative influence on your feelings. It also ensures that you do not attract the same experience again. I have shared this technique with many people over the years, and have always found it to be deeply powerful in the positive changes it brings.

Enjoying the journey

Focus on the journey, not the destination.
Joy is found not in finishing an activity but in doing it.

GREG ANDERSON

Life is filled with contrast. Everywhere you look and every-thing you experience helps to clarify what feels good and what doesn't. When you find something that makes you happy, do it more. This keeps your brain actively releas-ing bliss peptides. When you find something that doesn't make you feel good, take a step away and turn toward something that feels better. If life brings you something that you don't want, ask yourself the question, "What do I want?" Focus your mind and attention only on the things that make you feel good inside, and Source Energy will match those good feelings.

On your journey toward the life of your dreams, the universe will continually send you signs to guide you in the right direction. Many people are too busy concentrating on the road in front of them to notice these signs, but they are always there. A while ago my wife, Debbie, decided that she wanted to get an Apple MacBook. As she began to focus her attention on the idea of owning one, she soon began to receive signs from the universe to guide her. When she watched TV, she repeatedly saw MacBooks. Whether it was a documentary, sports program, or drama, there they were. When she looked in magazines, they were there again. If she talked with anyone about computers, they would invariably say how much they liked Apple's computers.

As she continued to dream of owning her own Mac-Book, she wondered to herself, "Which color shall I get, black or white?" This wondering flowed out to the universe, and it wasn't long before a good friend came to visit and brought her white MacBook with her. Debbie and she had great fun playing on it together. A week later, another friend came to visit from Venezuela with his black Mac-Book. The universe brought Debbie the contrast to experience, and from that she decided which color she wanted. At the same time, she learned lots of new things about MacBooks before hers even arrived.

The more she dreamed of owning one, the more signs she saw. After only a few months, she received some money unexpectedly and was able to buy the computer of her dreams. She loves it and has endless fun on it. Enjoy your dreaming and always be watching out for those signs from the universe. They arrive to remind you that the things you desire are on their way; so follow those signs and enjoy the journey.

No one comes to see me without having already followed the signs to find me. I never advertise, so all my clients find me through word of mouth. I do not heal anyone, instead I show clients how to activate their own healing by following the signs their body gives them. The body always wants to heal, and when we change something in our lives that promotes healing, the body always responds by reducing its symptoms of *dis-ease*. The change might be eating a different diet, taking an herb or supplement, or even just changing your mind.

———

Gina came to see me with a diagnosis of polycystic ovaries. This condition is linked to hormonal imbalance and can produce a variety of symptoms, including menstrual irregularities and weight problems. Gina's chief symptom was spots on her face. Although in her early twenties, her skin looked like she had a bad case of teenage acne. This made her feel very self-conscious and insecure.

I shared with Gina my understanding of the strong link between happiness and health, and recommended that she concentrate on doing things that made her feel good. I also suggested that she change her diet and take some supplements. Three weeks later, she came to see me and her skin was looking noticeably clearer. She also appeared to be much happier and more confident.

I asked her which of my recommendations she had followed so far. She told me that she had not yet managed to change her diet nor taken any supplements. However, after our first meeting she said that she had decided to focus her attention on things that made her feel good, and consequently, had been enjoying life a lot more. By being happier, Gina had activated self-healing and her skin was showing clear signs of this. Although eating a healthy diet and taking supplements can certainly aid healing, the most dramatic healing comes when we change our thinking. Gina began enjoying her journey through life and her body responded by showing her a clear sign that she was heading in the right direction.

———

Ancient spiritual traditions recognize that the universe is abundant with signs, and the interpretation of these signs has been practiced for thousands of years. There are signs to be seen in our interaction with the natural world and, in many traditions, animals, birds, and plants all have special meanings. Signs can be seen in the stars, clouds, unusual weather, and a host of other phenomena. There are also divinatory arts throughout the world, such as reading the tarot, casting runes, and consulting the I Ching. Signs can be found not just in ancient arts and the nature, but anywhere and everywhere.

Some years ago, I became interested in numerology, the study of the meanings of numbers. Each number from one to nine has a specific meaning; dates of birth and even names can be assigned one of these numbers. There are also special numbers, called *master numbers*, which have their own meaning. A master number is any number made up of repeating digits, such as 11, 22, 33, and so on. When a master number appears in your life, it can be taken as a special sign.

When I applied numerology to my name, it produced the master number 11. This number is linked to revelations and the uncovering of new perspectives. I found this interesting, especially because I am always looking for new perspectives. After this I started noticing when I saw the number 11, especially on digital clocks. I found that if at any time I doubted my path, I would see a clock displaying 11:11. It might be the clock on my laptop, on our VCR, on our cooker, or the clock in my car. I took this as a sign from the universe that I was on the right path and to trust my intuition.

The universe always gives me clear signs when I am heading in the right direction. When something special and unexpected is heading my way, I cannot stop seeing master numbers on clocks throughout the day. As I go through my day, I periodically check the time and will see 11:11, 13:13, 15:15, and so on. I now know that if I see more than three master numbers in one day, something that will greatly expand my bliss is about to arrive in my life. You might think that this is a bit "out there," but it works every time. Once you open your mind to the possibility of the universe guiding you, the signs will appear. Follow those signs and your journey to bliss will be simple and quick.

Happiness, health, and healing

Healing may not be so much about getting better, as about letting go of everything that isn't you—all of the expectations, all of the beliefs—and becoming who you are.

RACHEL NAOMI REMEN

Every day, part of you is brand new. The cells that make up your amazing body do not live forever. Some live for years, but others for only a few days. Your body makes millions of new cells every day to replace ones that are worn out or have finished their work. These new cells always match how you are currently feeling. As your happiness increases, you change the very makeup of your cells. Happiness is not only felt in our minds, but in every single cell of our bodies. A happy cell is a healthy cell, so naturally as you increase your feelings of well-being, the new cells you make will be healthier.

In his groundbreaking book, *The Biology of Belief,* Bruce Lipton explains how science is beginning to understand that when we change our beliefs and feelings, these changes are registered in our DNA, the part of us that holds the blueprint for making new cells. It has long been thought that we are controlled by our genes, but in fact the latest evidence suggests the very opposite. Genes are turned on and off by signals from outside of the cell, including our thoughts, emotions, and feelings. It seems that we are much more in control of our bodies than most of us realize.

Part of living happiness will always include having perfect health, and this is achievable by everyone. Happiness and health go hand in hand. As your level of happiness increases, so will your sense of well-being. You may currently be manifesting a health problem; it might even have been labeled as "incurable." But if that label doesn't make you feel good, don't believe it. The body will always heal itself given the right set of circumstances and feelings. The word "incurable" really means that no one else can cure you. If you want to find true healing, you always have to find it for yourself.

Every day, thousands of people are told that they have some kind of incurable disease. When people are given this label it has an immediate impact on their happiness. The body responds to how we feel, so just to be told that you are incurable will generally have a negative impact upon your health. There are, however, countless people living today who were given such a label but chose not to believe it. They decided to follow their feelings and look for better feelings every day, and in doing so, healed themselves.

Your body has incredible powers of healing and rejuvenation. Every moment of every day your body is seeking balance and harmony. Cells respond to good feelings and actively release anything that does not resonate with those feelings. Your cells work with the Law of Attraction, too. When you hold on to negative emotion, your body holds on to the toxicity that matches those feelings. This in turn attracts more toxicity. In many people, this attraction is felt as food cravings or drug dependency.

All dis-ease, as its name suggests, is a lack of good feeling. When you improve the way you feel, your body is capable of healing in a very short time. Gregg Braden, in *The Divine Matrix*, talks about the healing of a woman with an inoperable tumor in a matter of minutes. Three healers worked on the patient and held a vision of her whole and healthy. Within minutes, a massive tumor vanished. This might sound impossible, but Braden says it was filmed and documented. Healing doesn't have to take years to achieve. The moment you set your mind to being open to the possibility of perfect health, you start to attract new information and ideas to show you the way.

My dream health

Decide right here and now that you want to have perfect health. Write a wish list of things that would make you feel great in your body, such as boundless energy, good sleep, and perfect vision. Create a picture in your mind of how you want your body to be and then say to yourself,

"It is already done." Many people have healed themselves by consistently holding a vision of perfect health. Some say affirmations such as "Thank you for my healing" or "My body is in perfect balance." Activating the feeling of wholeness already achieved seems to bring about the fastest and most dramatic results.

Once you have created a vision of perfect health, provided you continue to work on ever improving your feelings, all manner of new opportunities and connections will come into your life to guide you back to health. Once you decide that health is your destiny, this intent is felt at a cellular level, and you will begin to feel your body respond when you connect with part of the answer you are seeking. The answer to all questions, including how to be healthy, lie within you, but sometimes you will attract someone else to remind you of what you already know.

We have a built-in sense of what is right for us—our intuition. Many people ignore it, but it is always with us and always active. The truth has a resonance that is sensed by everyone. We even talk about how something "rings true," like a bell going off inside our heads signaling that we have connected with something important. When you hear something that will help you with your healing, it will feel right. If you follow those feelings, they will lead you quickly and efficiently to wholeness. It might be something you read or a person you meet that gives you a whole new perspective. It might even be as simple as witnessing the energy of someone who is already whole and happy that inspires you to match them at a cellular level. Whatever it is, never stop believing you can have perfect health.

Happiness and light

People are like stained glass windows: they sparkle and shine when the sun is out, but when the darkness sets in, their true beauty is revealed only if there is a light within.

ELISABETH KÜBLER-ROSS

At a quantum level, our minds and bodies run on light and electricity. For some time scientists wondered why, when you tread on a hot coal with a bare foot, it takes a little while for your brain to realize the danger, but once you do, your response is almost instantaneous. The small time delay in the information reaching your brain is significant in contrast to the message to move your foot, which is immediate.

Why is that?

The message traveling up your body to your brain is electrical, but the message to move your foot is encoded in light. Nerves in the foot register heat from a hot coal and transmit this information electrically along a pipeline of nerves toward the brain. As this message is transmitted from one nerve to another across what is called "a synapse," there is a slight time delay. That's why it takes you a short while to register the danger. However, once your brain actually registers this danger, it encodes the message for your muscles to move into a biophoton, a subatomic particle of light encoded with your DNA. This travels down your body at the speed of light creating an instant response. Isn't that amazing?

We intuitively know that people who are at the top of their game emit more light. It's how we describe them. When someone excels at something, such as in sports or on stage, we talk about how they shine. We also speak of people glowing with health and describe children that do well at math as being bright. When you are happy, when you are in the right place at the right time and doing the right thing, you literally shine brighter. In her book *Cellular Awakening*, Barbara Wren shows how when we are happy and free from stress, we can hold more light around our cells. This light illuminates the ancestral wisdom that we each hold in our DNA.

To understand how we hold and use light in our bodies, we need to explore some of the fascinating scientific discoveries of the past fifty years. The story begins with the discovery of how living cells feed and excrete using the movement of two fundamental elements: sodium and potassium. Full scientific details can be found in a book called *The Salt Solution* by Herb Boynton, Mark F. McCarthy, and Richard D. Moore.

Every cell of every living creature, from the single-celled amoeba to the trillions of cells that make up you and me, has a mechanism within it called the sodium-potassium pump (abbreviated to the Na/K pump). This mechanism is very ancient and has existed since the dawn of animal life on this planet. The purpose of the Na/K pump is to move sodium ions out of a cell while moving potassium ions in. Without this mechanism, your cells would die. This process is so vital that up to a quarter of the energy you obtain from the food you eat is used to power these pumps. Scientists still do not know the full extent of their functions, but do know that they power the movement of nutrients and waste products in and out of the cell while supporting a wide variety of different cellular processes. This in turn affects your energy levels, pH, heart function, and your ability to heal. More recently, scientists have discovered that these cellular pumps affect your ability to hold light.

At nighttime, your body naturally moves into a mode of rest and rejuvenation. While you are asleep, every cell in your body uses the Na/K pump to pull potassium ions into your cells and push sodium ions out. Both of these ions are positively charged. For every two potassium ions that are pulled into the cell, three sodium ions are pushed out. This creates a difference in the charge inside and outside of the cell membrane (the cell wall). The outside of the cell becomes positively charged while the inside of the cell becomes negatively charged. This difference in charge is called your *cell membrane potential.* It is the battery that provides the power for all other cell functions to take place.

When the outside of your cells are positively charged, they attract negatively charged electrons that form clouds around the outside of the cell membrane. These electron clouds, in turn, attract and hold photons of light around the cell. Without these electron clouds, your cells cannot hold light, and without light they cannot fully function. When you are happy and relaxed, your Na/K pumps work efficiently and you literally shine with vitality.

The one thing that dramatically reduces our body's ability to hold light is stress. When we get stressed, our body changes from its normal functioning into fight or flight mode. Massive chemical and hormonal changes unfold as adrenaline pumps through our bloodstream. One of the chief side effects of stress is dehydration, and this is felt by your body at a cellular level. Our cells are made up mostly of water, and without it, a cell cannot function. When you become dehydrated, your cells protect themselves against fluid loss by impregnating their walls with cholesterol. Cholesterol acts as insulation and prevents further fluid loss. The main side effect of this insulation is that it reduces the effectiveness of the Na/K pump. This changes the electrical charge around your cells, reducing their ability to build up a strong outer positive charge, and therefore, reducing the formation of electron clouds. This in turn reduces the amount of light around each cell.

Everyone knows that stress is not good for us, but few realize the potential implications it can have on our happiness and health. Stress is the number one cause of all illness, and it often arises because we are resisting something or someone. When you do not resist what comes into your life, there is no stress. The happy person is naturally relaxed and goes with the flow. Their cells are fully charged, and they shine with a vitality that everyone can see.

There are many things you can do to increase the amount of light you hold, but being happy is the most fundamental of all. There are also supplements you can take, such as oils containing omega-3 and omega-6, that are rich in electrons and photons. If you want to know more about this fascinating subject, I recommend you read Barbara Wren's *Cellular Awakening*.

The 5 keys to a stress-free life

Tension is who you think you should be.
Relaxation is who you are.

CHINESE PROVERB

Happy people tend to not get stressed. When they do, they quickly turn it around so they can return to their natural, happy state. The stresses of modern living are one of the chief causes of unhappiness in our society. Stress has two fundamental causes: resistance and contradiction.

When we are resistant to situations that we don't like it causes stress in our minds and bodies. If we view the mind as the scientist and the body as the lab, whatever the scientist chooses to focus on dictates how well the lab functions. Contradiction comes when we compromise who we are in order to do something we don't want to, but feel that we must. Contradictions make us feel like we are being pulled in two different directions. This in turn causes an imbalance in many of the chemical reactions taking place in our lab. We can guard against stress by following a few simple guidelines.

1. *Always be yourself*

When we are not true to ourselves, when we act in ways that are contrary to our character, a contradiction is always set up inside of us that results in stress. Some people hold a host of different characters within themselves. At work they are one person and at home a completely different character. With their friends they might be another and with their parents, yet another. People often do this as a coping mechanism when faced with situations that could potentially make them feel uncomfortable. They change character in order to feel better or to blend in. They try to bring balance and harmony to their external environment in the hope that it will make them feel better. This coping strategy never leads to true happiness, only temporary relief. If you want to bring balance and harmony into your life, you must first find it within.

The other problem with this coping strategy is that often one character suddenly appears at the wrong time. Someone might be very controlled at work, but angry at home. Sooner or later that angry character will reveal itself at work. When this happens, people can end up hating or resenting certain parts of their own psyche. Self-hate is one of the biggest contradictions we can hold. Fundamentally, we are love, and loving oneself is so important when creating happiness and harmony.

The answer to this is to simply always be you. The trick to achieving this is to learn to wear many different hats. I wear all sorts of hats. I wear the writer's hat, the lover's hat, the teacher's hat, and the pupil's hat. I am a father and a son, a gardener and a woodsman, a dreamer and a doer. The world presents us with a rich array of contrast, and the only way we can effectively navigate through this and remain happy is if we always remain true to who we really are. Wear lots of different hats, but let the person wearing them remain the same. Do not try to change yourself in order to please others. The only work of true change is within.

When you are true to yourself, your unique personality shines out for all to see. Your heart is open and your beauty overflows onto those around you. You might think that your true self is angry or fearful, but this is not the case. At your core you are divine: pure love, compassion, and understanding. Negative feelings and emotions only arise when we step away from who we really are. As you work on living happiness, the true you will reveal itself in absolute beauty. You are an amazing, special, unique human being. You were born to shine your light to the world so that all who see you stand in awe. That's who you really are. Be happy and you will find it easy to always be yourself. Always be yourself and you will find it easy to be happy.

2. Give not a care to what others think of you

This step is intrinsically linked to the first step. We are only not ourselves when we are trying to please others or fit in with what we think they want. The moment you care about what other people think of you, you will stop being yourself. This does not mean that you don't care about other people—you just don't care about what they think of *you*. It is how you feel about yourself that really matters. You and only you are responsible for how you feel, and it is the same for everyone else. How we choose to react to others always reflects back to us. It really has nothing to do with them. The Law of Attraction says that only similar feelings are attracted to one another. This means that you cannot attract being hurt by anyone unless you are already carrying unresolved pain inside of you.

Whether you see the best or the worst in others depends purely on whether you see the best or the worst in yourself. Life is a mirror, and what we do not like in other people is only ever a reflection of something we do not like about ourselves. It may be hard to accept, but this is a great gift because it allows us to become aware of where we need to balance our lives. It gives us the opportunity to look within and release the things that don't make us feel good. When you are connected to happiness, you are connected to your divine self and you view everyone with compassion. When we judge others, we close our hearts, and in doing so, we diminish our happiness.

As you walk on this path of ever-increasing bliss, you will inevitably change. Some people will embrace this change, but others may resist the new you. If you care what others think about you, you will tend to hold back on change, and in doing so, hold back on your happiness. If you want those you love to find ever deeper levels of happiness, care only about how you can improve your own feelings. By uplifting your own spirits, you show others that they too have the power to find their own happiness. Perhaps this is the greatest gift you can give them.

3. Temper your preferences

If you want to be always living in happiness, do not like anything too much or dislike anything too much. When we have strong preferences, we become very vulnerable to stress. If you like something a lot, sooner or later it will most likely disappear from your life, and this will cause you the pain of loss. Likewise, if you dislike something a lot, sooner or later it will arrive on your doorstep and cause you stress. Only the person who holds no strong preferences can remain happy in all situations. This is not to say you shouldn't have preferences. Indeed, they are essential for steering a true and happy course through life. We are naturally attracted to things that make us feel good and steer away from things that make us feel bad. Only the very strong preferences are dangerous.

Zen Buddhism teaches that we should hold onto nothing and let nothing go. When wonderful things come into your life, treat them as if a beautiful butterfly had landed on the palm of your hand. Marvel at its beauty, sit in appreciation of it, and when the butterfly wants to fly away, watch it fly off and be happy for it sharing that moment with you. By taking this opportunity, you open up new possibilities for even more beauty to flow into your life. If you try to take hold of the butterfly, you will most likely injure it and its beauty will not be able to inspire others. Let everything sit in the open palm of your hand and allow things to come and go as they please. In doing so, you remain forever free to be you.

4. Get creative

When you are creative, whether it is physically or mentally, you open up a powerful connection between you and Source Energy. You become a channel for divine inspiration. Creativity expands your consciousness, illuminates your brain, and sends more light into your cells. You cannot be stressed and truly creative at the same time. Creativity is the very opposite of stress. A happy person always makes time to be creative every day. The creative process is an important part of ensuring that happiness continues to flow from and through us.

When we are creative, we awaken the parts of our consciousness that form the foundation of our reality. Moment by moment, our thoughts and feelings create our reality. The reality we experience is a pure reflection of what we have first created in our minds. When you create something beautiful in thought, word, or action, you will see that beauty reflected back to you. Write a poem, paint a picture, dance and sing. If you don't feel you are naturally creative, why not take a class or two and explore new parts of your being? Creativity can come from so many different sources.

Your greatest source of creativity is your imagination. It is the power behind happiness. Setting and mending your day (see pages 65 and 70, respectively) are both powerful creative processes. The next time you find yourself facing a challenge, don't get stressed, get creative. Let your imagination start you on a journey to places that inspire bliss. Play the *wouldn't it be nice* game to connect with solutions, and if you simply follow your good feelings, everything will always turn out fine.

5. *Meditate*

Everyone I have met over the years who is happy and successful, practices some form of meditation. Meditation clears the mind and allows inspiration and wisdom to rise up from our subconscious. We hold all the answers we seek within us. Often people are too busy thinking to allow the space for those answers to rise to the surface. Meditation creates this space within our minds. The benefits of meditation are immense. When you practice meditation, your heart rate and breathing become slower and calmer. This normalizes blood pressure and increases oxygen levels throughout the body. This in turn boosts your immune system and increases serotonin production, which naturally lifts your mood. Meditation increases creativity, boosts self-confidence, and even stretches time. People who meditate actually have more time in their lives as a result of being more relaxed.

Meditation can be as simple as sitting or lying in a relaxing position while focusing your mind on your breathing. As you sit, allow thoughts to flow in and out of your mind without taking hold of them. This might be challenging at first, but becomes easier with practice. One of the best ways to get the most out of meditation is to exercise beforehand. When we exercise, a biochemical shift takes place within the body. Exercise increases your metabolism, flooding your blood and brain with oxygen. This increases your mental clarity. An oxygenated brain creates a rich palette for the art of meditation. If you exercise and then meditate afterwards, you will be amazed at the wonderful new ideas and creative processes that form in your mind.

A simple meditation: Sit or lie comfortably with your eyes closed. Focus on your breathing. When you breathe in, imagine light flowing into your lungs and body. When you breathe out, imagine your whole body relaxing. Practice this for five minutes one to three times a day. Each time you practice, you will be allowing your mind and body to find deeper levels of harmony.

Sleep changes your mind

If you have an important decision to make, or if someone has upset you and you feel compelled to confront them, it is always best to wait until after you have had a good night's sleep before acting. After sleeping, you will always see a different perspective, and more often than not, you wake up with a clearer understanding of the best course of action.

When we sleep, our body goes into a healing and balancing mode. Sleep is the body's natural time for housecleaning. Dead cells are cleared away and taken via the blood and liver to the intestines to be excreted. The blood is filtered and cleaned, and any damaged area of the body is flooded with all the necessary ingredients for perfect repair. After a good night's sleep, the freshly cleaned blood is able to carry extra oxygen to the brain and other organs. When this happens, we wake up feeling refreshed with a new, clearer perspective on life.

Our minds also go through housecleaning while we sleep. Negative thoughts are often released through dreams as our subconscious mind is busy sorting out all the challenges and problems that we are currently facing. If I have a problem for which I cannot find a solution, just before I go to sleep I ask my subconscious mind to work on it over night. Invariably, I wake up the next morning with a solution clear in my mind. When I am writing, I program my subconscious to think about the next chapter while I am sleeping. When I do this I always wake up with new ideas in my head.

The next time you have a decision to make and are sure you know what to do, sleep on it. If you wake up with the same surety, follow that decision. If, on the other hand, you wake up with a different path in your mind, sit with it for a while so that you can gauge how you feel about it. If it feels right, go with it. If you are unsure, sleep on it a second night. The morning always brings a fresh perspective.

Make life your playground

A three year old child is a being who gets almost as much fun out of a fifty-six dollar set of swings as it does out of finding a small green worm.

BILL VAUGHAN

Do you still know how to play? Playing is a great way to connect with your inner happiness because there is a part of you that always loves to play. It is your *child side*—an important part of who you are. Many people forget or ignore it the moment they start to grow up, but happy people naturally allow their child side to play every day. Young children are fascinating to watch and can teach us many lessons about living happiness. For them, life is an adventure of discovery, and their feelings are their guide.

Children tend to do only what makes them feel good, but only for as long as it is enjoyable. A young child will pick up a new object and be enthralled with it. Their senses take them on a journey of discovery as they look, smell, touch, and taste this new thing. They may play with it for a long time or a short while, but you can guarantee that the moment it no longer feels good, they will immediately let it go without a care and move onto the next thing. They do not worry when they let something go that it will be lost forever. They simply and effortlessly move into a new experience.

Children are wonderful demonstrators of enjoying the here and now. They are always in the moment. When a child first learns to walk, a whole new phase of discovery in life begins. Standing up and walking to somewhere new, a child finds a new place that is always different from the last one—and is filled with new experiences to discover. A toddler has no care about the route taken and no worries about what this new place might hold. The toddler is just in the moment, enjoying the adventure. Through movement, play, and exploration, a child's brain develops and its neural net becomes fully activated. When we continue to play and explore throughout our lives, life is a fun-filled adventure.

Excitement and enthusiasm are natural byproducts of playing. As you play, your brain releases bliss peptides. All your body systems resonate with these positive feelings and work at their optimum efficiency. When you are having fun, your whole body feels great. Your mind is free of negativity and your spirit soars. Soon you're having such a good time that it overflows from one plaything to another and from one person to another. When you are having fun, Source Energy brings to you an endless stream of experiences to further expand your enjoyment of life.

Fun always brings laughter, and there is nothing better for your body, mind, and spirit than laughing. Research has shown that when people laugh, their bodies' powers of healing and rejuvenation are enhanced. Laughing strengthens the immune system, reduces food cravings, increases one's threshold to pain, and protects against heart attacks. Indeed, there are healers and teachers whose main work is in reminding people how to laugh. Many people have found that laughter has enhanced their ability to heal. Laughing creates a wonderful physical and emotional release. The art of happiness is the art of having fun.

Pets are good for your bliss

Having a pet, especially a cat or dog, is a great way to give yourself blissful feelings on a daily basis. Stroking a cat or playing with a dog activates the pleasure centers in your brain, flooding your body with bliss peptides. A pet brings out your caring side and rewards that care with companionship and unconditional love. Many people with long-term depression have found their spirits lifted by owning a pet.

Our cat, Simba, seems perfectly bioengineered to bring Debbie and me bliss. Every day she comes to us for love and affection. When I am writing, she often sits on my lap while I type on my laptop. If I am not sure what to write next, I stop and stroke Simba for a while. She purrs with pleasure and together we sit bathing in blissful feelings.

It is very relaxing to sit quietly stroking her. As I relax, invariably a new idea arises in my mind. Simba ensures that throughout my day I take time to rest and relax with her. When she comes to me for affection, I take it as a sign from the universe to take time out and bathe my cells in bliss. If you have the time and space, owning a pet can be good way to further activate good feelings within you.

The snowball effect

Success comes from taking the initiative and following up … persisting … eloquently expressing the depth of your love. What simple action could you take today to produce a new momentum toward success in your life?

ANTHONY ROBBINS

When you draw together your understanding of both the art and science of happiness, you begin moving swiftly toward a bliss-filled life. When you focus on what you want, you get more of what you want. This increases your bliss and expands your consciousness. Soon you will be experiencing the "snowball effect." If you begin to roll a snowball down a hill, as it progresses it attracts more snow to itself. This increases its size and makes it roll faster. Soon the snowball has become so big and gathered so much speed that there is no stopping it. It is the same with living happiness.

If you work with the tools in this book and concentrate on things that make you feel good, very soon a stream of matching, good-feeling experiences will begin flowing into your life. Before you know it, every day will bring you an endless stream of wonderful experiences, incredible surprises, and amazing miracles. Life will just get better and better, and those around you will marvel at your seemingly effortless ability to consistently manifest good things into your life.

The snowball effect is about having such a great ride down the hill that you effortlessly fill your snowball with all the happy feelings you find on your way. And you know that you are going to reach to bottom of the hill soon enough, so you enjoy the fun of the ride. When you do reach the bottom of the hill, there is a gentle and graceful feeling of bliss beyond what you ever expected. Wow, you feel great. You had so much fun creating your happy snowball that you just want to do it all over again, and you do. You just start another snowball right there where you are. You don't even have to climb up to the top of the hill again. Your positive thoughts mean that you are already there and all set to start another wonderful collection of good-feeling thoughts.

Once you have an idea and give it just a little attention, it begins to roll down the hill of life gathering to it, by the Law of Attraction, similar feeling ideas. The wonderful thing about the snowball effect is that once it is started, it takes care of itself. All you have to do is enjoy the ride. Soon you will find that whatever you desire comes your way with ease.

Happiness is a state of mind, but more importantly, it is truly a state of feeling. It is our inner happiness that allows us to flow through life with joy. Being in a blissful, loving place is the most delicious feeling. It's like connecting with all the energies that we truly are, like being free to fly to whatever gives us joy. Start imagining what you want. Be creative and let those feelings of bliss gather momentum. Just keep adding to them every day, and very soon you will be enjoying the best ride of your life—filled with fun, laughter, excitement, and joy. That's the snowball effect!

Sharing Happiness

Shining your light

*Happiness comes when your work and words
are of benefit to yourself and others.*

BUDDHA

Recent research indicates that it is better to give than to receive. Even the simplest acts of kindness increase our happiness. Elizabeth Dunn from the University of British Columbia (www.psych.ubc.ca/~edunn/index.htm) conducted a study in which participants were given $20 and told to spend it that evening. They were randomly divided into two groups. One group was told to spend the money on themselves while the other group to spend it on a gift for someone they cared about. The group that spent the money on their friend or loved one showed significantly higher levels of happiness afterwards.

Feeling happy is wonderful, but it's even more wonderful to share that happiness with others. When you uplift another person, both of you feel the benefit of that connection. A sure-fire way to further increase your own happiness is to help another human being connect with their own inner joy. We cannot make another person happy—that is their own responsibility—but what we can do is to offer them the opportunity to choose a path that feels better. Just being happy and open-hearted in the company of others has a strong, positive effect.

Scientists at the Institute of HeartMath (www.heartmath .org) have been studying many different mind-body connections. In a series of groundbreaking experiments, they discovered that the magnetic field of one person's heart can influence the brainwaves of another person in the same room. The heart generates the strongest electromagnetic field of any of the organs within the body, including the brain. The strength and coherence of this field increases when a person is in a caring and loving state. When two people come together in close proximity, the electromagnetic waves generated by one person's heart can positively influence the other person's brainwaves.

Under certain circumstances (i.e., when the "sender" is in a peaceful, happy, and loving state), the brainwaves of the "receiver" become synchronized with the heartbeat of the sender. In other words, people with a more coherent heart rhythm are more likely to influence another person's brainwaves. This means that by just being in a room with another person while feeling happy, loving thoughts, you can positively influence that with your heart's magnetic field.

We are much more interconnected than most people realize, and when we are happy, our light not only illuminates our own wisdom, but also brightens up the lives of others. Sharing happiness is about inspiring those around you to raise their consciousness to higher levels, to see a bigger picture, and to realize their own incredible power to create a wonderful life for themselves. It opens an awareness to the possibility of improving how they are feeling right now. One of the easiest ways to do this is to always be optimistic.

When someone expresses to you that they are not feeling good, making them aware that they can feel better is a great gift. However, this is not about preaching to others, it is just about offering a brighter and lighter perspective. "It will all work out fine in the end," "Don't worry, you'll find the answer," and "I know you can come through this" are the kinds of words of encouragement that, when delivered with grace, can be of great comfort to people who are feeling down. Just making them aware that their current situation can have a positive outcome opens their minds to new possibilities.

When someone is stressed or in turmoil, providing a little relief can make a huge difference. For example, some years ago I was in a shop, standing behind a young girl who was about to pay for two items. The shop assistant scanned the items and said to her, "That will be £3.95."

"But I only have £3.90," she replied. The assistant sighed with impatience.

"It's £3.95! If you haven't got enough then you'll have to put one item back. Which one do you want?" The young girl was in turmoil. She clearly wanted both items and could not decide which one to leave behind. I watched as both she and the assistant became increasingly agitated. She couldn't make a decision and the assistant was getting evermore impatient. At this point I reached into my pocket, pulled out a five-pence piece, and handed it to the girl. The look of relief on her face was instant. She thanked me and handed £3.95 to the assistant, who also looked relieved now that the problem was solved. The girl left the shop smiling, and all three of us felt lighter. The cost? A mere five pence.

We all want the world to be a better place, and you can start just by being kind to others. If you can make a difference in the lives of the people you meet, you can make a difference in your community. If you can make a difference in your community, you can change the world. Some years ago, someone created the slogan "Perform random acts of kindness." This message quickly caught the imagination of others and spread from one person to another. Someone printed it on business cards and began handing them out.

Soon the slogan was traveling around the Internet, inspiring people to be kind to others. All sorts of wonderful things happened as a result. People started paying for the next person at toll booths; some paid for another's parking ticket, and others tipped ordinary people who were not normally recognized for their work. A wave of positivity swept across America and Europe as the message spread. Now there are books, organizations, Internet sites, and even radio shows devoted to making the world a better place through performing random acts of kindness.

You have absolutely nothing to lose by sharing positivity with others, and everything to gain. When two people come together and share bliss, the magnetic radiance from their hearts goes out into the universe. It is like a beacon that makes the world brighter and lighter. Try it for yourself and see just how good it makes you feel. Do something kind for someone today. Why not smile at everyone you meet? Shine your light and inspire all you meet to do the same.

Freedom and allowing

The amount of happiness that you have depends on the
amount of freedom you have in your heart.

THICH NHAT HANH

Wouldn't it be nice if from this moment on, with every passing day, you felt a steadily increasing sense of bliss? Happiness can became your natural way of being and grow to such a depth that no circumstance will rob you of it. Just by being your true, blissful self, you will inspire everyone you meet. It feels good to imagine the world being a better place, but it feels even better to see it coming to pass right before your very eyes. Remember, if you can imagine it, you can make it real.

Blissology offers us the opportunity to experience living in peace and harmony. At this point, there is a tendency to ask questions, such as "How can we make this happen?" and "What must I do?" Remember, the "how" is the work of Source Energy. Your only responsibility is to be happy. "Surely if I want world peace, I must form or join some organization that campaigns for peace?" The answer to this is, "Only if it feels good for you to do so."

When you are happy, everything you do becomes easy. Life becomes a pleasure. The world around us is a reflection of the thoughts, feelings, and emotions we express in our daily lives; so if we want harmony in the world, we must first find it within ourselves. My promise to you is that as you find more peace and harmony within your own being, you will see more peace and harmony in the world around you.

Everyone wants to be free; nobody wants to be a slave. We all want to be free to think how we want to, to not have anyone or anything force us to think or act in ways that don't feel good. For most of us, when we were children, our parents acted as our guides. They told us what to do and what not to do. This important training allows us to be able to safely navigate through life without coming to harm. "Don't run out into the road." "Always look both ways before you cross." "Be careful." "Don't touch that, it is hot." Throughout our childhoods, we are endlessly told what we can and cannot do.

However, there comes a time, when children start to question what they have been told and yearn to make their own decisions. This "change of mind" is an important part of growing up, and later on, most children leave the nest and fly out into the world on their own. From here on, they and they alone are responsible for how they think and what they choose to give their attention to.

If you want to be free to think and choose, you have to allow everyone in the world the same right—even if their viewpoints and values are the polar opposite of yours. The moment you say, "You are wrong," you are beginning to exert your will upon another person. What you put out is what you get back, so if you seek to tell others what to do and how to think, sooner or later you will find someone doing the same to you.

When you discover a better way of being, there is a tendency to want to tell the whole world about it. The danger here is that in doing so, you start telling people what they should and shouldn't do and how they should and shouldn't think. This rarely makes other people feel better, especially if they haven't asked for your opinion. If you give someone a piece of information that they are not ready to hear, it will serve no purpose. It is with our optimism, enthusiasm, and happiness for life that we can guide others toward seeing a different perspective.

Allow everyone the freedom to be who they are. Your only work is to shine brighter. As you increase your own sense of happiness, those around you will notice it. Sooner or later, someone will come to you and ask, "How come you are always so happy?" Now is your opportunity to open your heart and share your wisdom because their questioning indicates that they are be willing and open to hear what you have to share. The act of sharing means selflessly giving a part of yourself to another while asking for nothing in return. Sharing is wonderful because it makes everyone feel better. If we want the world to be a better place, if we want people to understand how to be happy and free, we must imagine it first. Wouldn't it be nice if it was not hard to change the world? Dream that dream.

Holding your integrity

Integrity is the essence of everything successful.

R. BUCKMINSTER FULLER

In a village in China, there lived a blacksmith with his wife and daughter. At the other end of the village was a Buddhist monastery. The blacksmith was very possessive of his daughter and held very traditional beliefs.

"One day soon I will find you a good husband, and when you are married you will have a fine family of your own," he would often tell her.

His daughter didn't like the idea of her father choosing her a husband, especially as she was already in love and having a secret relationship with the carpenter's son. One day she realized (to her horror) that she was pregnant and she knew that if her father found out he would be very angry. Fearing for the safety of her lover, she decided to try to keep the pregnancy secret. She took to wearing loose clothing to hide any signs of the baby growing inside of her. One day, however, when she was only a month away from giving birth, her father noticed her large bump.

"What's that?" he roared, pointing to her tummy. "You are pregnant! What fiend has done this to you?"

The daughter, wanting to protect the man she loved, blurted out, "It was the abbot in the monastery. He got me pregnant."

The blacksmith stormed out of the house, walked all the way through the village and into the monastery. There he found the abbot kneeling peacefully in meditation. He pulled the abbot to his feet by the scruff of his robe and said, "You have got my daughter pregnant. When this baby is born it will be your responsibility. You must look after it because you are the father."

"Is that so?" replied the abbot.

"Yes," said the father. With that he stormed out of the monastery.

Four weeks later, the blacksmith's daughter gave birth to a beautiful baby girl. The blacksmith wrapped the newborn child in a blanket and took her to the monastery. This time the abbot was sitting and teaching a group of young monks. Once again he pulled the abbot to his feet, and thrusting the child into his arms said, "This is your child. You are the father. She is your responsibility."

"Is that so?" replied the abbot.

"Yes," said the blacksmith, and off he went back home alone.

As the next few days passed, the blacksmith's daughter was missing her baby so much that she decided to come clean and tell her father the truth. "The baby is not the abbot's," she told him, "It is the carpenter's son. We are very much in love. We want to get married and bring our child up together."

Her father was enraged. "How could you do this to me?" he said. Once again he stormed out of the house and to the monastery. This time he found the abbot feeding the baby some goat's milk. He snatched the child from the abbot saying, "This is not your child. You are not the father. She is not your responsibility. I am taking her home with me."

Once again the abbot smiled and replied, "Is that so?"

"Yes," said the blacksmith, who then took the baby home to its parents.

This story is one of my favorites because it always reminds me just how easy it is to hold your integrity. At any time, the abbot could have leapt to his own defense, but instead he just practiced acceptance. When the blacksmith first came to him, you might think that he would be perfectly justified to defend his good name. He could have said, "How dare you disturb my meditation. Don't you know who I am? I am a holy man and have taken a vow of celibacy. How dare you accuse me in this way?" Instead the abbot, knowing his own truth, simply replied, "Is that so?"

When the blacksmith returned with the baby girl, the abbot could have said, "I told you that you have the wrong man. We cannot have a baby in our monastery. It will distract the monks from their meditation. Besides, it's a girl, and females are not allowed in here." But the abbot again simply accepted this new opportunity. He took the baby with an open heart.

When the blacksmith returned a third time to take the baby away, the abbot could have said, "You can't have her. We have bonded and I know I will give her a better life than your daughter can. It's not fair for you to take her away." But once again, he practiced perfect acceptance, just saying, "Is that so?"

Holding your integrity means remaining happy and true to yourself no matter what is going on around you. Happiness brings with it self-confidence, faith, and trust. When you believe in yourself, you know that you can access all the resources and wisdom you need to navigate any situation with ease. When you trust your unfolding path, it is easy to hold your integrity. With self-belief comes the faith that everything that is coming into your life is for the expansion of your bliss. Nothing is wrong and everything is right. However, when unexpected challenges come our way, we can lose our sense of self, and, thus, our integrity.

Old patterns of behavior can emerge and rob us of our bliss, but only if we react in the wrong way.

There are two basic ways human beings react to unexpected situations: as a potential threat or as an opportunity for growth and learning. When we feel threatened, our body goes into protective mode. We become more contracted and our biochemistry prepares for fight or flight. In other words, we feel stressed. It is impossible to hold your integrity if you view anything or anyone as a threat. When threatened, we naturally become defensive, or even aggressive.

When we see a challenging situation as an opportunity for growth, our body goes into assimilation mode. We become more expansive and our biochemistry prepares for new input. Our brains light up, activating new neural networks. When you stand in your truth, you have an inner knowing that everything you attract into your life is for the greater good. When you seek only to find the good in everything and everyone, even apparently negative situations turn out to your advantage. Unexpected challenges can feel great, especially when we find within us the ability to overcome them with ease. Even the most outlandish and unexpected turn of events can simply take you deeper into your inner knowing and expand both your consciousness and happiness.

The positive sandwich

*The positive thinker sees the invisible, feels the intangible,
and achieves the impossible.*

AUTHOR UNKNOWN

There are times when we feel the need to tell someone
something that has potential to make them feel bad. Many
people carry sadness within them, and when unexpected
events or bad news come their way, they can lose sight of
the positive. Although we know it is not our responsibility
to make others happy, we can help them navigate challenging times by offering the opportunity to see a brighter
picture. Bad news does not have to cause unhappiness.

Whenever I have something to share with someone
that has the potential to upset them, I use a technique I
call *the positive sandwich*. I start by helping them to focus on the positive, briefly share the potentially negative
information, and then end the conversation on a positive
note again. Positive sandwiches are great. I use them not
only to help others, but also to ensure that I, too, always
look on the bright side. Motivational speakers, managers,
and popular political leaders all use this technique to help
people feel good, especially in challenging situations.

A great way to create a positive sandwich with others
is to start and end with appreciation. People love to be

appreciated, and it always activates their inner bliss. Positive sandwiches are designed to help a person connect to their heart, so what you say has to be kind but also honest. Here are two simple examples:

- *I can't come to your party*—"I'd love to come to your party. Thank you so much for inviting me. Unfortunately, I can't come this time, but I will be thinking of you all having a great time together. I will be with you in spirit, sending you lots of love. I know you'll all have a great time."

- *I'm breaking up with you*—"I am so glad you came into my life. We have had a great journey together. I know that in your heart you always want the best for me. You want me to be happy and that's what I want for you, too. I feel that I need to go and seek that happiness on my own, so I am breaking up with you. I hope you understand and will love me enough to let me go. I know that in the end this will be best for both of us."

No matter what you have to say, it will always feel better if you place it in a positive sandwich. Positive sandwiches guarantee that both you and those you converse with will always have the opportunity to give their attention to positive, good-feeling thoughts.

Teaching from behind

The art of teaching is the art of assisting discovery

MARK VAN DOREN

We live in a society where we send our children to school to be taught what we believe to be essential skills for life. They learn to read and write, which are very important because the written word is a powerful source of information and insight in this modern age. They also learn to add, subtract, multiply, and divide, which are vital skills in a society where money is so central. They also get to share a wide variety of experiences through music, drama, sports, and other recreational activities. However, while schools can definitely enhance our range of skills and knowledge, most teaching does not take place in school. Most of the learning we do as both children and adults is through our social interaction.

Children begin learning by interacting with their parents and extended family. Much of this teaching is done subconsciously. When learning language, children follow their parents' example and try to mimic their sounds and emotions. Parents add extra emotion to certain words to help their children learn the feelings behind those words. For example, food is portrayed as a happy, positive sound, while danger is portrayed in a much more forceful way.

This helps children understand that food feels good and danger feels bad.

When children are learning how to talk, they learn so much more than just the meaning of the words. Behind every word is an emotion. If a parent holds a lot of fear within them, much of that fear will be passed on to their child just by their example. I saw this process in action very clearly when a mother and child came to see me some years ago.

I received a telephone call from Elizabeth, who was obviously very concerned about her seven-year-old son, Johnny. She told me that he kept falling over. This had been going on for several weeks. She felt that something was wrong. The next day she came over with Johnny. He appeared to be a healthy, normal young lad. I examined him and asked him to do some simple balance tests. His eyes, ears, and breathing were all normal, and he had excellent balance. I told Elizabeth I could find nothing wrong with him, but that perhaps if we let him play in the garden, I might see something new that would explain this problem.

Our garden has two large lawns, and on one of them some delicate spring flowers were growing. Johnny ran onto this lawn and dodged in and out of all the flowers at great speed. He was clearly having fun and enjoying himself. What was interesting was that he managed to avoid treading on every single flower despite his speed. There was clearly nothing wrong with his coordination. After a short while, he ran over to a rockery, and began climbing on the rocks. Again his balance and dexterity were excellent. Elizabeth had been talking to me when Johnny first ventured onto the rockery and it was only after he had been playing on it for some time that she noticed him.

"Johnny, be careful!" she suddenly shouted. The young lad jumped with the shock of being shouted at. He lost his footing and fell over.

"See," said his mum, "I told you he had balance problems."

Her fear of him falling was expressed through her words to him. He felt this feeling, which threw him off balance emotionally and subsequently manifested as him falling over physically. There was absolutely nothing wrong with little Johnny. The solution to the problem lay with his mum. Once I was able to show her this, she changed the way she spoke to him when he was playing, and his falling over stopped.

We have far more responsibility for the teaching of our children than perhaps we realize because most of what children learn is through our example. In Zen, it is called "teaching from behind." Children learn more through the feelings that flavor your words than from the words themselves. This is true for everyone you meet. The most powerful way you can help others is to embody the very solutions they are looking for. If someone is agitated, rather than shouting, "Calm down!" it is far more helpful for you to embody calmness. When you are calm, you show and share a resource that will help them to feel better. If you want to help people to have happier lives, teach by example. Teaching happiness from behind is always of far more value than merely talking about it.

A life beyond your dreams

People are inherently capable,
aspire to greatness, and have the power to choose.

FRANKLIN COVEY

Happiness and the life of your dreams can be yours. You *can* feel better with each passing day *and* be continually thrilled at your own ability to create wonder and magic in your life. My sincere wish for you is that from the moment you first picked up this book, your imagination has been kindled and set alight. That those dreams you had when you were a child can be, if you choose, realized in your own lifetime. What's more, new dreams can continually arise to be fulfilled. You can make your life the way you want it to be. Create a life of fun and adventure for yourself, and in doing so, you will have given the greatest gift you can to all those you love and care for. You will have shown them the way—demonstrating that if you can realize your dreams, so can they.

If you set your mind toward a better life, very soon you will find yourself living a life beyond your dreams. As you feel evermore blissful, the universe, through Source Energy, will bring to you unexpected things to match those feelings. This takes you even deeper into the expansion of your joy and appreciation. Source Energy, our Great Sea of Love, knows that you love good surprises, and is eagerly waiting for you to bring yourself into alignment with bliss so that it can shower you with them. You will meet new and inspiring people, visit places you never knew existed, and have forever-expanding feelings of joy that make every moment of every day a thing of beauty for you.

I dreamed of you reading this book. I imagined you reading it and understanding its simple message. I opened my mind to the possibility that *you* can have a better life—that your feeling of inner well-being can grow and expand beyond your wildest dreams. I imagined you so filled with bliss that everyone you meet remarks on it. It is my dream for this message to travel around the world so that everyone begins to understand the power we hold in our minds and hearts to discover deep happiness. This book is my personal invitation to share in that dream with me. You have so much to gain from doing so. You *can* make a difference. What you do and how you think and feel is molding the future right now. Wouldn't it be nice if that future was filled with hope, aspirations, and love?

There has never been a more exciting time to be alive. The world is changing fast, and with this change we have the opportunity to become the artists and sculptors for the generations to come. In the future, people will look back at this time and sit in awe at the great work that was achieved by their forefathers. You are part of that great work. Happiness is waiting for you around every corner. As you travel through life, experience the contrast between what feels good and what doesn't, then do only what feels good. In this way, your sense of happiness and well-being will always continue to grow and expand. Follow your dreams and never accept that second best is okay. You were never meant to just make do—you were meant to be amazing.

When new opportunities arise, embrace them with open arms, for they will take you closer to the realization of bigger and better dreams. Follow your intuition. Know that you are the master creator of your own reality. Know that happiness, health, and fulfillment can be yours forever. There is no limit to what you can do and achieve. No matter what your age, no matter what situation you find yourself in, improvement can come to you right now.

I trust that as you have read this book, your own level of happiness has increased. I know that as I have written it, my own bliss has deepened. Play with the tools and ideas I have shared with you because they can have a profoundly positive effect on your life. I have used many of them for more than two decades and am continually amazed at how magical and powerful they can be. I have seen people locked in sadness suddenly find freedom and joy; those with incurable illnesses find miracles of healing that at one time they believed were impossible; and I have seen despair change to hope, doubt to faith, and hatred to love.

Human beings are the most amazing creators, and when someone truly commits to a better way of living, the change in their magnet of attraction is instant. As you work with these simple ideas and share them with others, the life of your dreams will come to you. As you expand your happiness and creativity, new possibilities will continually arrive for you to play with. You will feel the interconnectedness of everything in this amazing universe and know that anything is possible if you only take the time to dream.

Your life up until now may have been a mixture of both positive and negative experiences, but from this moment on it can be forever different. You can rewrite your story in a way that continually brings you happy endings. Happy endings give birth to happy beginnings again and again. A wonderful sense of well-being and grace flows through you, coursing through your blood and into every cell. When you follow your bliss, you cannot help but feel better with each passing day. Life's rich tapestry of experience gives each of us the opportunity to choose who and how we want to be. Remember, happiness is always only a thought away.

Bliss is your destiny. It is your continual birth right and can be claimed at any moment. So step forward boldly and know that you can make a difference. You are special, unique, and beautiful. You deserve to see that beauty in everything you do. We each make our own reality, so why not make yours one that thrills you and fills you with bliss? There are so many wonderful new things for you to experience in your life ahead. I sincerely wish you deep and lasting joy. The best is yet to come.

Expect your every need to be met.
Expect the answer to every problem,
expect abundance on every level.

EILEEN CADDY

Further Reading

Baggott, Andy. *Living the Zen Arts*. London: Octopus Publishing, 2005.

Batmanghelidj, Dr. F. *Your Body's Many Cries for Water*. Los Angeles: Global Health Solutions, 1994.

Boynton, Herb, Mark F. McCarthy, and Richard D. Moore. *The Salt Solution*. New York: Avery Publishing, 2001.

Braden, Gregg. *The Divine Matrix: Bridging Time, Space, Miracles, and Belief*. New York: Hay House Publishing, 2007.

Doidge, Norman. *The Brain that Changes Itself: Stories of Personal Triumph from the Frontiers of Brain Science*. New York: Penguin Books, 2008.

Emoto, Masura. *The Hidden Messages in Water*. Hillsboro, OR: Beyond Words Publishing, 2004.

Godefroy, Christian H. *Super Health: How to Control Your Body's Natural Defences*. London: Piatkus Books, 1992.

Hicks, Esther, and Jerry Hicks. *Ask and It Is Given*. London: Hay House Publishing, 2005.

Lipton, Bruce. *The Biology of Belief: Unleashing the Power of Consciousness, Matter & Miracles*. Santa Rosa, CA: Mountain of Love, 2005.

McTaggart, Lynne. *The Field: The Quest for the Secret Force of the Universe*. London: Harper Collins, 2001.

Pert, Candace. *The Molecules of Emotion: The Science Behind Mind-Body Medicine*. New York: Simon & Schuster, 1997.

Sykes, Bryan. *The Seven Daughters of Eve: The Science that Reveals Our Genetic Ancestry*. London: Corgi Books, 2004.

Wren, Barbara. *Cellular Awakening: How Your Body Holds and Creates Light*. London: Hay House Publishing, 2009.

To Write to the Author

If you wish to contact the author or would like more information about this book, please write to the author in care of Llewellyn Worldwide and we will forward your request. Both the author and publisher appreciate hearing from you and learning of your enjoyment of this book and how it has helped you. Llewellyn Worldwide cannot guarantee that every letter written to the author can be answered, but all will be forwarded. Please write to:

Andy Baggott
c/o Llewellyn Worldwide
2143 Wooddale Drive
Woodbury, MN 55125-2989

Please enclose a self-addressed stamped envelope for reply,
or $1.00 to cover costs. If outside the U.S.A., enclose an
international postal reply coupon.

Many of Llewellyn's authors have websites with additional information and resources. For more information, please visit our website at:

www.llewellyn.com